DE PROFUNDIS

OUT OF THE DEPTHS

FRED PIETROWSKI

outskirtspress
DENVER, COLORADO

Outskirts Press, Inc.
http://www.outskirtspress.com

ISBN: 978-1-4787-2536-7

Outskirts Press and the "OP" logo are trademarks belonging to Outskirts Press, Inc.

*I dedicate this book
to my wife Linda of 50 years,
and to my loving family.*

*Ed Collins, my right hand man,
without his help this book would not be finished.*

*The Salem New Hampshire writers group,
whose coaching and encouragement
helped make it happen.*

*My life experiences are shared by
many other submarine veterans.
"We were never there" means
no medals can ever be awarded
for above and beyond
"the call of duty."*

Table of Contents

Mission Statement

The following account tells of my life aboard the World War II diesel submarines, the *USS Angler SS240* and the *USS Entemedor SS340* during the Cold War. I recount some of the everyday events, which I experienced in the *Silent Service*. A life of intense, high drama, unseen beneath the waves, my story tells the true facts of many life-threatening events, that I survived from 1959 to 1964.

We were to become a part of history in the making, warriors too young to realize the impact of our service, not just for our country but for the whole world.

Frederick Pietrowski
Electrician Mate, Third Class Petty Officer Controller Man (SS)

CHAPTER 1

A Glimpse of Things to Come

Upon entering the Navy, and after boot camp, I was chosen to attend the Naval Electrical School program in Great Lakes, Illinois. While there, I volunteered for the Submarine Force, which started the long selection process by which I became part of the *Silent Service*. Neither I, nor any of my peers had any idea what our lives would be like living in a sixteen-foot-wide steel tube submarine. The tight space we called home had 125 sailors aboard with beds for only sixty-six men. An empty bunk from someone on watch became yours with three, two-foot-long bags of each man's belongings hanging on the side of the bed. Sharing was the rule we lived by, whether space or the air we breathed. We bonded and became family, closer than brothers.

Our sub performed secret missions, often releasing thirty-six mines or twelve frogmen, while still submerged.

Once while standing on watch topside, we entered New York City inner harbor in the spring of 1961. I spotted three Russian submarines hiding next to the Statue of Liberty, only one half mile away from Wall Street. Our submarine base in New London, Connecticut sent five other diesel boats to help us. We were ordered to ram the nuclear sub, trapping it in shallow water, so we could get all their latest high-tech equipment.

During more than three years stationed at the submarine base in New London, Connecticut, I came to learn the real meaning of *hazardous duty pay*. On July 21st, 1961, while I was driving our boat, we were rammed by a super oil tanker that cut our sub in half, which sank to the bottom of Long Island Sound.

In the fall of 1961, we dove into an uncharted, fresh water stream-layer, and dropped like a rock three hundred and seventy-seven feet crashing into the ocean bottom off Rhode Island.

In the spring of 1962, a two-inch wide pipe exploded, flooding and trapping me in the Control Room compartment as the sea rushed in.

I was almost eaten by a shark twice, once being circled by a thirty-five foot Great White for six hours in the wide, open ocean, and the other time after being knocked overboard on top of a sixteen-foot shark, which I escaped by climbing on top of a torpedo that we were reloading at the time.

In October of 1962, we lived through the Cuban Missile Crisis while fighting hurricane *Ella* in the North Atlantic. The storm's rogue wave rolled us almost completely over to 57°, leaving us in total darkness with no power. My job as forward electrician watch was to crawl in the dark, over pipes and valves, and return power to save the ship.

In the winter standing on lookout in the North Atlantic, I survived the freezing waves coating me in winter-white ice, with icicles hanging off my eyebrows and mustache.

In another incident, we were submerged on patrol in tropical waters, and had to breathe in the 125° to 140° heat for three weeks. It burned our noses to try and breathe through it, we had to inhale through our dry mouths.

Our submarine hunted in the depths for any telltale sign of a target. When located, like a shark, we emerged from the depths and struck our target, silently returning to the depths undetected.

History should tell what submarine life is truly like from one of those *Silent Service sailors*. Hollywood often depicts a mottled, undisciplined crew, but in reality, we were highly trained to survive. On a submarine, a serious mistake by one could mean death to all.

CHAPTER 2

Flash Back

I was standing on the submarine bridge in Long Island Sound, watching the nervous, young faces of the officers in training. It brought me back to the time a year earlier, when I first volunteered for submarines. I was enrolled in the Naval Electrical School in Great Lakes, Illinois, and saw a note posted outside of the barracks labeled Submarine Volunteers Wanted. I heard that only one out of a hundred people that applied became a submariner. Ever since I was young boy, I've always enjoyed swimming beneath the water, and watching the fish move about in their own world. I was more at home under the water, than I was on top of the water.

On the next day, I headed to the designated building, and a third class petty officer clerk brought me to speak with an admiral.

His dark, blue jacket was covered with rows of rainbow-colored, battle ribbons, topped by his shiny, gold dolphins, which was the badge of a submariner. We spoke for a while, and then he asked me, "Why do you want to be in submarines"?

I said, I loved being underwater, and would be proud to be a submariner. He told me to wait for orders.

Soon those orders came with my first test to try and enter the Submarine Service. I reported to a large brick building, and was immediately sent into a ballroom-size, blackened room with only a light on over a wooden desk. While walking toward the desk, a voice boomed out of the darkness, "What do you like more, boys or girls"? I froze in disbelief.

"Girls, sir."

My mind was racing by the abruptness of the unseen inquisitor. I sat in a chair in front of the desk barely able to see the man questioning me. He was a Naval psychiatrist and continued to ask questions in quick succession for over an hour. I came to learn that this was the first of five sessions, which were conducted by five different psychiatrists.

When I completed my studies at the electrical school, an officer came to our classroom, and gave each of us five choices of where we could be assigned. He read the locations out loud: "Pearl Harbor, Hawaii, San Francisco, California, Bubble Gum, South Africa," we all laughed—there is actually a base called Bubble Gum. Bubble Gum was a three-man radio station out in the middle of the bush with a signal tower and motor generator set. Thirty days out in the bush, back for a few days, and then back out for thirty more days. On a lark, one unlucky sailor picked Bubble Gum as his fifth choice and, you guessed it—off to Bubble Gum, South Africa he was headed.

My orders arrived—three years shore duty at the submarine base in Pearl Harbor, Hawaii! Wow! I rushed to tell all my friends, and they cheered with me for my good news. Then, an old timer on base said to me: "Too bad for you. Hope you love cheap beer; sailors don't make much money, and Hawaii is expensive." When we got paid and went into town, the women would flock all over us. But after a few days, when we ran out of money and were all broke, the women left us and returned to their local boyfriends. Meanwhile, all we could afford afterwards was a case of cheap beer to drink on a lonely beach.

I quickly did what I could to get my orders changed to submarine school in New London, Connecticut. Luckily for me, I was sent to New England.

When my two weeks leave was over, I reported to the submarine base ready for the next levels of tests to enter the submarine service. I joined the other sailors at the sub school barracks, and waited for the many mandatory physical tests to begin. None of us had any idea what the tests were, what they would be like or how many we would have to endure. The barracks were full of hopeful sailors from every background and physical size. We all waited and dealt with our anxiety, playing cards or lying on our cots in-between work details.

Before long, each one of us was called and sent in different directions for testing. Now, we had to take the physical tests in *"the tank and the tower."*

My 24-man group was sent for the first test, conducted in a large building on the lower submarine base. Before the test began, the instructors explained how to depressurize our bodies, so our ears would not rupture and we would not get the bends.

We were brought into a large open space, where I saw a round cylinder about eight feet in diameter called "the tank." There were small windows all around it, and a hatch to get in. Protruding from one side was a steel bubble with its own inner and outer hatch. It would be used if someone in the group could not adapt to the pressure inside. The instructor would take that sailor into the little side container and close its hatch. The instructor would then slowly depressurize him to prevent the bends. The rest of us would continue to have the pressure increased, until it matched the hundred foot depth pressure, 133 pounds of pressure per square inch on our bodies.

Finally reaching that depth pressure, we started to smile, all of the holding of our noses and popping of our ears forgotten. One of my classmates began to speak, and he sounded like Donald Duck. We all started laughing, creating an entire family of quacking ducks. It was quite the scene; twenty-four men sitting on the floor of an eight-foot cylinder in three lines, hundreds of pounds of pressure on our bodies, quacking like a flock of ducks.

Our first physical test was completed, we sighed with relief. Just one more physical test to go!

CHAPTER 3

The Submarine Base and the Tower

I walked around the Submarine Base in New London, Connecticut. Everywhere about me were historical artifacts from World War II. I saw a two-man, Japanese World War II submarine in front of a brick building. It was cut open, and I could see the inside short periscope and batteries. This submarine was carried by a larger submarine to invade Pearl Harbor. When close enough, it was released with the two submariners inside. It headed for the mission at full speed. It was a one-way trip. Success or failure was determined by the destruction, and a ball of fire from their launched torpedoes.

A large round brick building kept the war records of the most famous World War II submarines. On the walls were pictures showing their battered condition after returning from heroic missions. Underneath them were colored war ribbons, they earned during those battles. Pictures above showed submarines torn apart, after being depth charged for a long time. Another submarine had torn up its teak deck planks for masts, and had sewn together blankets to make sails. They sailed five thousand miles across the Pacific Ocean undetected and returned home! Their engines were all damaged, but the crude sails brought them through rough weather and unbearable heat.

Then, I saw the USS Angler SS240 picture with its many battle ribbons. This submarine went into shallow water to a remote island in the Philippines on a rescue mission. It evacuated nurses and children from under the nose of the Japanese. The submarine dark colored hull was an easily seen target from above against the sandy ocean bottom. The Japanese depth charged it over and over, but she sneaked away into the depths. Over fifty other submarines were not so lucky, and never returned; they remained on "Eternal Patrol." They gave the ultimate gift to keep our nation free.

On the next day, I had to go to the dreaded hundred foot tall "tower." It was a silo just twenty-five feet wide and filled with water. This water tower taught us how to escape from a submarine. Twenty-four of us marched into a classroom beside the tower. We learned how to swim up fifty feet to the surface on a breath of air. We were all a little scared. If we didn't perform this skill correctly, we would get the bends and be crippled or killed. I listened as the experts described exactly how to escape from a submarine. Twelve of us at a time went into an elevator on the side of the tower, and rode down fifty feet. When the elevator door opened, the instructor reached over and unlocked the tower outside chamber hatch. Inside the white chamber was a large, chest-high ring in the middle. We climbed inside and looked at each other, as the instructor sealed the hatch! We prepared for the flooding water to rush in through the perforated holes in the floor. The instructor said "ready," and turned the small center valve and water started rolling and bubbling though the holes in the floor. I watched as the water crept up my legs, and slowly inched up my chest onto my chin. My head was in an air pocket less than a foot from the top of the tank! I could feel the pressure in my ears, and pressing all over my body. The outside water had compressed the air in the chamber to the same pressure as our fifty-foot depth. I had to suppress the urge "to get the hell out of here". I kept thinking breathe, calm down, just calm down. I fought the fear of drowning, and my breathing slowed down. I took a deep breath and let it out; took another deep breath, let it out; took the last deep breath, and held it. I swam over to the inside center opening, and dove down through the underwater hatch. I looked up at the fifty-foot column of water above me. The circle was twenty-five feet wide, but looked like the size of a shimmering dime. There were safety divers every ten feet, staggered all the way up to the top to watch my assent. I started blowing out my air like whistling, staying below the pancake-size bubbles forming above my head. I was taught to stay below the bubbles or I'd get the bends. I rose up toward the surface, pushing up or down with my hands, to stay below the bubbles. Fear of the bends or running out of air filled my mind, as I ascended! The divers watched me intently, as I passed each one. Their job was to stop anyone who panicked. If anyone thrashed toward the surface, the diver had to catch him! Then, punch him in the stomach, pushing out all his air and preventing the bends. They forced the panicked student into an air pocket behind them to calm him down. Then, the diver brought him to the surface sharing an air tank.

The bends is a condition, in which nitrogen bubbles build up in your blood, crippling or killing you. At fifty feet, my lungs held three times the volume of air it held at the surface. I got rid of all my extra air long before reaching the surface. My mind was spinning as my head broke through the surface, and I took a deep breath. The instructor grabbed me and said, "Face the wall," watching me closely. I saw the rest of my group pop up one-by-one, untill all had surfaced. The instructor turned to me and said "One more time."

He wasn't sure if I'd expelled all the air out of my lungs. Fearfully,

I set off and traveled down the elevator through the hatch, and let the water creep up onto my chin. I went through the breathing, the expelling air and ducking through the hatch. I blew those pancake-size bubbles, and never wanted to go through that again. I made sure all my air was out long before I got to the surface! The sound of my lungs filling echoed everywhere. I thought, that they could hear my inhalation echoing all the way off base to downtown New London, Connecticut.

I heard of one sailor a few weeks before me, who had panicked and fought off all five safety divers on his way to the surface. They rushed him to a high-pressure hyperbaric chamber, and he spent hours slowly being depressurized. The chamber got most of the nitrogen bubbles out of his blood, but sadly not fast enough. He lost the use of his legs, and was washed out (discharged) from the Navy.

I still dream and relive that fear I felt in the tank to this very day! I never wanted to do that again—never ever again!

CHAPTER 4

Life as a Lookout and Encountering a King

Mess Hall

Upon graduating from submarine school, I was assigned to the hunter killer submarine the *USS Angler SS240*. During my first three months, I was a mess cook, helping to prepare the five daily meals. The long hours and lack of sleep showed the rest of the crew, that I could handle the stressful life in our sixteen-foot wide, steel-tube world.

During a storm, I started to prepare a meal by going down into our refrigerator to retrieve some food. I lifted the foot-thick hatch and latched it onto the wall beside, and started down the ladder into its middle. After three steps, I had to rotate around onto my heels and put my hands behind me to descend. I took another step and all of a sudden the sub lurched forward, tossing me against the hatch and unlatching it. The force of the sub's bow coming up threw the hatch into me, which forced my feet off the ladder and left them dangling in the air. My butt slammed down onto the hatch, crushing my two hands beneath me. With my feet kicking in the air, I pushed down with my weight letting my heels reconnect with the ladder. I pushed up freeing my hands, and leaned against the hatch to relatch. Then, I climbed up onto the deck, and saw to my horror that the nails of both my hands were torn almost completely off. All eight finger nails looked like baby-open clams hanging by their quicks. Soon, the full feeling would be returning into my hands, so one by one I started tearing off each nail before the total feeling returned. I was allowed to take a couple of hours off, then back to work washing the dishes by hand for 125 men. It made my hands burn, and brought tears to my eyes. I earned the respect of the crew that day, as I continued to work the eighteen-hour days, until my three months of mess cooking were done.

My next assignment onboard was as a lookout. The primary function of a lookout was spotting contacts, that the radar missed due to the up and down wave action or target size.

Our main function was protecting the boat from small, float-ing objects, or spotting things at a distance. However, the role involved working in different places at different times. At sea, I worked four hours on watch and eight hours off, seven days a week. On the eight hours off, I worked my specialty as an elec-trician. Other lookouts worked their specialties, like torpedo or engine-men. In the little remaining free time, we cleaned up the ship, ate, caught up on qualifying for my silver dolphins (gold is for officer).

During the four hours on, lookouts rotate jobs each hour. We go below to steer the boat by compass, or look through the periscope for objects. When submerged, the job was to keep the submarine on depth using either the bow or the stern diving planes. In port, we took turns standing watch for four hours next to the gang plank, which was our main entry point but restricted access to anyone unauthorized.

The most intense part of my job was out at sea. While the sub was on the surface, we would stand through a waist-high metal hole in the submarine's superstructure, exposed to the elements and standing only seven feet above the ocean. During hur-ricanes and storms, we wore seven layers of clothing with a six-inch, canvas belt around our waist, and a four inch leather belt on top. The belts were connected to the submarine by three chains. These three life lines—two forward and one aft, kept us from being pulled overboard by the waves underwater in the storm's fury. Wind-driven waves rose to over a hundred feet high, and crashed down completely engulfing us. Each time, I held my breath until the crashing waves cleared my mouth. I'd take a breath and then blink quickly before the forming white ice sealed my eye lashes together. Like candles being dipped, we became icebergs while the dripping water formed white icicles on our eyebrows and mustaches. I prayed to die many times, unable to stand the burning, cold, penetrating my face.

On warm days, it was a completely different experience. I have seen things a naturalist would die to experience. With the sun on my face, I watched dolphins dive beside or over the sub's bow or flying fish sail across the wave tops.

One morning, in the silver light of predawn, our submarine was bobbing up and down, charging the batteries. Every once in a while, I could hear splashing sounds all around the submarine, but I could not see what was creating the sound. When it got brighter, I discovered we were in the middle of a school of whales. Surrounding us were hundreds of whales spread out from horizon to horizon in every direction. Mother whales were with their calves in one area; a short distance away smaller "teenagers" were frolicking around. The older larger females were swimming together in a pod off by themselves. These aunts shared babysitting duties when their mothers dove deep for a meal, to return and nurse their multi-ton babies.

The sun slowly peaked over this wonder of nature as the dominant whale appeared, slowly swimming around his entire harem. All of a sudden, he spotted the submarine right in the middle of his family. He turned and came straight toward the middle of the sub at ramming speed! His tail was slapping violently against the water surface, whipping it into white foam as he raced across the top of the ocean. At the last possible second before contact, he dove under us and surfaced close up by our other side. He sped away out to four hundred yards, banging his tail all the way. The bull circled, and when abreast of us, turned, racing back at us again.

I could see the water spraying off his head, as his tail kept slapping against the ocean, and then he dove under us again. The monster surfaced just past our opposite side, and went out to three hundred yards. He circled like a bull with a matador, charging and diving again, each time getting closer than before. He then surfaced, and stopped very close by to study us. I felt we had just been challenged, his bowling ball size eyes staring right at us.

Was he wondering who or what was in the middle of his group? This huge bull whale had to figure out, if we were another male trying to steal his harem. The submarine was round and black with fins in the front and back just like another whale.

The weathered warrior finally decided that we were not a threat, and slowly swam up and started to rub against our side. His nudge shook our 2400 ton boat violently from side to side, and I wondered if we were being invited to join his group or was this the start of a mating ritual? We were trapped in the middle of this giant aquarium, unable to go in any direction. Moving could wound one of them, and instigate an attack by the whole group.

I watched the king with his 'Crown of Scars', and wondered what life stories he must have. Whales have to fight giant squids hundreds of feet below us. Many whales have washed ashore after these encounters with large battle scars. I've seen a whale with a three-foot-wide sucker mark on his side. On the ocean surface, the king must defend his group from many dangers. Dangers that include other males trying to take his harem, or starving sea creatures trying to grab a meal.

The balloon rubbing sound echoed out from our speaker in the sonar room below. This familiar sound I have heard before from many other whale encounters. The king was talking to the group, and soon they gathered and began to swim away. They traveled their ancient path off into their world, over the horizon, still unknown by man.

CHAPTER 5

Photo Ops and Mishaps

On a warm summer day in 1961, the *USS Angler SS240* was submerged in Long Island Sound heading home outside the Gold Star Memorial Bridge to New London, Connecticut.

The captain raised the periscope to look around before surfacing, and spotted a large tour boat coming down the Thames River. He could see tourists hanging over the side of the double-decker craft, staring at our periscope that was emerging from the water. The tour boat swung in a wide circle so the passengers aboard could take photos of our periscope.

The captain was in a good mood, so he announced over the speakers "Prepare for an airless surface." An airless surface meant racing the sub up to the surface without blowing water out from our ballast tanks. We would burst out of the water up into the air, then open the vents and let the water drop out of the bottom of our ballast tanks. Then, we'd quickly slam shut the air vents, trapping air inside the tanks.

Captain, then said, "Let's give them a real show."

We turned on a parallel course to the tour boat, and increased to full speed. "Prepare to surface," the captain called out. "Surface, surface, surface," blared from the 1mc mike system speakers. He ordered me and the stern planes man to put full rise on our diving planes. The ship's klaxon (horn) sounded arooga, arooga, arooga, and we zoomed to the surface. We came smashing up out of the ocean, spraying water everywhere. The chief of the boat, Soupy Campbell, opened all the main ballast tank vents, and water cascaded out of the bottom of the submarine. When the sub was two-thirds out of the water, the vents were closed trapping air in the tanks. We crashed down on the surface sending huge waves outwards in all directions. The tourists were having the time of their lives with all the action right next to them. Our submarine turned in a sharp circle at full-speed leaning way over. We started our diesel engines with a big roar, and a puff of smoke. The captain, myself, and the other lookout went up onto the bridge, and waved to all the flashing cameras.

I felt like a movie star and wanted to cup my hand, and give a royal bow to the cheering crowd.

The pilot on the ferry must have been taking in the sights, as well, because we suddenly heard a huge bang then a crunching sound. The bow of the ferry crashed, and was firmly imbedded by a large, Volkswagen-size sea buoy. I could see the anchor chain attached from the buoy's bottom rolled on its back on top of the ferry. The heavy chain was pulled taught, holding them both fast to the ocean bottom. Our sub rushed over to offer assistance, and to check if the ferry was sinking. Fortunately, they weren't taking on any water. No one was seriously hurt, and we stood by until a rescue ship came. A Coast Guard buoy tender ship finally showed up, and maneuvered to cut the heavy chain away. The heavy duty crane on its back lined up to lift the buoy off the ferry's crushed-in bow. The front of the ferry popped up when the weight was freed.

We followed the ferry behind the Coast Guard ship. We tried to do a good deed, but ended up causing thousands of dollars in damage. However, the tourists loved it, more fun than a Disney ride—excitement, panic, and then relief. They had quite a story to tell with the pictures to prove it.

CHAPTER 6

Eat My Dust

Many school ops missions ended on a Friday, and all submarines surfaced about the same time in their assigned areas. All of the football-field-long, black submarine bows surfaced, and got ready for the great race home. The crew were like kids, and we loved to play games. Just like NASCAR, we jockeyed for position and the race was on. Each submarine was at sea for one to three weeks, and the crew dreamed of the time off with friends and family. The first submarine in got an unobstructed path to land at the pier. The next sub had to wait for the first sub to moor and tie up, then the next for him, and so on. Sometimes, it took hours before the junior officers banged their ways into or beside the pier. Typically, there were five or more submarines with inexperienced officers heading home into the narrow channel.

One Friday afternoon, we surfaced in our area and saw the other "boys/subs" all spread out for the "Friday Night Fights." Like the Chariots of Old, we all joined the race rounding the coast from the east and west, or heading straight up the middle. I heard our engines roar to top speed, as we raced off with the others. I was the port lookout, and could see all the submarines spread out heading into port. It felt great with the wind blowing through my blond hair, squinting with the unaccustomed sun on my face. We were well ahead of the other submarines, and knew we had a good chance at winning this day. Everyone raced wide open before forced to funnel in together in the narrow channel. I felt like I was on a speed boat, yes, a speed boat. A foot ball field long, 2400-ton, steel speed boat. Everyone started to close in on each other, but we were still too far apart to make out the other faces. We entered first into the channel slot. Our ship's horn blared out the command to the train bridge ahead of us. Hoonk, hoonk! Open up for the USS Angler, the number one fastest in the fleet "eat my dust, guys!" We waited, but the train bridge didn't rise up, so we sounded the horn again, hoonk, hoonk. The sound now echoed off the buildings and the bridge that were closing in fast around us.

Like a circus train, all five submarines were weaving, strung out behind us, going as fast as they could. I watched the train bridge getting closer and closer, but still no reply from its operator's horn. We listened for their returning toot, and the lifting of the bridge for us to pass. I looked through my binoculars at the bridge, and saw a train starting to come across. We all were in big trouble with the pedal to the metal, and five multi-ton boats right on our tail. The captain yelled down to the men on deck, "attention on deck. I am going to cycle the vents."

A loud boom sounded as the vents opened, and water sprayed up in the air all over the sailors on deck. The sub dropped down a couple of feet, another plume of water, as we dropped down again and again. Finally, the deck was even with the ocean and splashed waves over it. We rammed forward, pushing most of the water out of the narrow channel exposing the rocky shore line.

The train traveled across the bridge overhead, as we splashed the waves up and over the banks down below. This exposed the bridge supports less than twenty-feet away on either side. One by one, each submarine behind us followed, scraping their bottoms on the almost empty channel. Any mis-alignment would take out the bridge, and bring the train down on top of us and into the sea. Once clear of the bridge, we blew the water out of our tanks, and rose up to our normal height. We traveled toward the submarine base with all the *barnacles scraped off our belly*. The deck crew was wet but safe.

CHAPTER 7

Rammed, Cut in Half, and Sunk

In the summer of 1961, our captain, Lieutenant Commander William Evans backed his hunter killer submarine, the USS Angler SS 240, away from the piers in New London, Connecticut. Our crew of 125 men got ready to travel down the Thames River. As we approached the train bridge that blocked our path to the sea, we sounded our ship's whistle. We heard the responding short toot from the railroad bridge operator, and the train bridge rose up. Sailors scurried about the narrow deck to secure everything, as we headed out to sea.

All three of our 16-cylinder diesel engines revved up, and waves started to splash over the bow and sides. The officer of the deck stood atop our bridge, with me the starboard-side lookout and another to port. The officer searched the horizon all around the submarine and yelled, "prepare to dive!"

His voice echoed in the crisp salt air. "Dive! Dive!" The ship's klaxon sounded the two blasts—*aoooga aoooga,* which means dive the boat. The foaming white sea sprayed up through the cracks in the teak deck. A loud boom sounded as the air escaped from under our deck, while the main ballast tanks filled with seawater through their open bottoms.

I ducked out of my lookout hole; turned, and dropped down twelve feet through the deck hatch. I was guided by my fingers against the back of the ladder to the conning tower room deck. Turning again, I dropped another twelve feet, and landed in the control room. The other lookout quickly joined me. The deck officer took a last quick look around, and dropped down to the conning tower below. He quickly jumped up, and grabbed the hanging lanyard rope handle on the deck hatch, and fell back pulling it shut. Then, the quartermaster leaped up onto the ladder, and spun the center wheel to finish sealing the deck hatch. The officer spun around, and dropped the last twelve feet to the control room floor.

Facing my diving station, I looked at the array of levers, buttons, and gauges that controlled the depths and the submarine angle. I turned on the power to rig out the bow planes, and spun my wheel to full dive. When the boat dive angle reached five degrees, I maintained that angle; if the ship's angle became more severe, the whole deck would act as a wedge and we'd dive straight down into the bottom. During storms, it is very difficult to maintain the angle and depth with the force of the waves constantly crashing down.

There are four people in each lookout group, two for the diving planes, plus one steering and one to man the periscope. On the surface, the two on the diving planes become lookouts. We worked a four-hour shift, rotating the jobs every hour and then taking eight hours off. During the eight hours off, I worked in the electrical field, while others worked at their specialty whether it was torpedo man, sonar man, or engine man.

On this particular trip, we had twelve junior officers to train. They each had to trim (balance) and dive the boat, execute an attack on a ship, and fire a practice torpedo. The opponent destroyer was twenty-five miles away, and ran a zigzag course trying to find us. In each exercise, we fired a torpedo under the keel of the destroyer while he searched for us. If the destroyer located us first, they would drop a practice 10-pound depth charge—assuming they were lucky enough to find us. We would send up red flares to indicate a direct hit, which happened only twice in hundreds of attempts.

After we surfaced to get fresh air and rotate the watch section, I began steering our course at the helm. I looked in front of me at the compass repeater. It had a 6-inch slot behind the compass, which held a multi-sided plastic disk for secret missions. This disk tricks the internal gyro mechanism from the true course. Around the helm are gauges to indicate rudder angle and speed levers to make a change to individual propellers. Hanging by my right shoulder was the ship microphone. Overhead were three alarm levers: general, battle and collision. They were painted yellow, green, and red respectively, with each handle knob a different shape to identify them in the dark.

On this mission, we slowly approached our target like a cat creeping up on a mouse. We wanted to remain undetected, until close enough to fire a torpedo at the destroyer. The torpedo internal gyroscopes were set to pass ten feet below the destroyer keel. When right on target, we saw their ship send up a red flare through the periscope indicating a killing shot—game over. We surfaced, retraced the fired path, and retrieved the torpedo to reload and to repeat the procedure with a different officer.

In one war game, a practice depth charge dropped so close to our submarine, that it shattered the light over my head and showered me with glass. The impact of the blast lifted me off the floor like the first hill drop on a roller coaster. It was just a 10-pound depth charge, but in war, they drop 500-pounders.

Things do go wrong. I have seen submarines coming into port with gaping holes through their superstructure, high splashing waves spilling over a torpedo sticking out of their side!

On secret missions, no one aboard ship knows where we actually are going, not even the captain. Everyone just follows the written preplanned directions with a special blue-colored numbered chart. No land or depths are indicated on the chart, it's only covered with numbers.

"Battle Stations!" ordered Captain Bill Evans. "Battle Stations, aye!" I replied, mindful that you must always repeat commands to avoid a mistake. I turned the battle station alarm handle. "Bong! Bong! Bong!" The sound rang throughout the ship. Sailors ran by each other to their assigned stations, and several young trainee officers came up into the conning tower.

The small oval conning tower was packed tight with the extra personnel. I stood at one end with the captain; to my left was the periscope operator. On the other side, there were the six junior officers spread around in a semicircle with the navigator and executive officer. Everyone was in a space smaller than the size of a car. If someone wanted to scratch, somebody else had to move.

Lieutenant Junior Grade Brian Shea was in charge of the attack. Our phone talker said to the captain, "All compartments manned and ready, sir." The junior officers took their battle positions around the conning tower, with several manning the torpedo data computer. Lieutenant Shea was on the periscope with another student calling out the target bearings. A junior officer was on the light table tracing our course. Lieutenant Shea called out, "mark" from the periscope, and another trainee gave that bearing to be marked on the chart table. The navigator drew a line from the light dot on his table that indicated our route out to the target sighting. A speed rule was laid across these many lines, which indicated the target speed and direction of travel. Every two minutes, Lieutenant Shea raised the periscope and turned to the last known bearing.

I knew exactly how much pressure these officers were feeling. On a previous secret mission up north, I drew the lines on the plotting table tracking 135 different targets, and calculated as fast as I could each one's direction and speed.

The captain stood to one side watching all of the junior officers; he only interfered in case of an emergency. The submarine turned and started to close the gap on our target. The periscope could be up no more than fourteen seconds, or it would be detected by the destroyer radar. Up and down the periscope went, recording bearings as the officers analyzed the data before firing a torpedo. After a few minutes, the captain called out to Lieutenant Shea, "When was the last time you raised the periscope?" Lieutenant Shea replied, "it was four minutes," and the captain reprimanded him for taking too long.

Lieutenant Shea said "the destroyer had turned into a small, rolling fog bank".

"Maybe the destroyer saw a flash when the periscope was turned," said the captain, who then ordered "up scope," and turned it to find the destroyer. Instead, he saw an unknown *huge gray ship's hull* right on top of us!

The captain yelled to me, "All ahead emergency! Ring the battle, general, and collision alarms! Pass Collision Eminent Conning Tower" on the one MC microphone. My hands were pushing and turning handles, while alarms echoed throughout the ship.

The captain yelled down to the control room below, "Flood the after tank group, put a bubble in the forward main ballast group!" The floor hatch beside my foot slammed shut. The back of the submarine dropped and the front rose as we lurched forward. I heard a loud crunching sound as something rammed into us. We rolled wildly to our right and shuddered. I could feel and hear the boat being torn apart. The sounds of metal crunching and tearing echoed throughout our boat as something crashed down the length of the submarine. We dropped stern first into the depths of the Atlantic.

Down and down we dropped, faster and faster, as more pipes were torn open, filling with sea water. Officers and sailors were thrown down onto the conning tower deck, but I hung on tightly to my steering wheel. The sounds of the alarms clanging and bonging in our small space were deafening. We slammed into the ocean bottom stern first with a loud crunching noise. The bow banged into the sea floor with a loud, echoing metallic ring. We listed to a radical angle to the right to an unknown depth.

The captain yelled to our phone talker, "All compartments report damage!" One by one each compartment called in. Luckily only minor leaking and flooding was reported. The captain ordered the floor hatch beside me opened.

All hatches throughout the ship are closed in a collision to reduce flooding. The chief of the boat was on the hydraulic manifold and yelled up, "Green board, sir!" This meant none of the deck hatches had been sheared off. The captain yelled to the auxiliary manifold man, Don, "Blow safety, negative and the main ballast group tanks!". This would reduce our weight and hopefully let us rise toward the surface.

Don put the handle onto the valve stems and released air from our 3,000-pound air pressure tanks into the main ballast tanks. Instead of hearing a bubbly sound of water and air escaping, I heard a hissing sound—then all went quiet. We were *trapped* on the ocean bottom, so deep we couldn't blow the water out of our tanks.

There was no panic, because panic meant death. All I could think of was "What can I cross-connect or do to offset the collision damage?" With our current 125-man crew, we only had eighteen hours of air to breathe. During World War II, the submarine carried a maximum crew of sixty-six.

I thanked God that there was no flooding in either battery well. Each battery well had 126 1-ton batteries; each filled with thirty-six gallons of sulfuric acid. If salt water leaked and mixed with the acid, forming chlorine gas, one whiff would mean instant death.

The captain and his officers conferred in the conning tower.

Don was ordered to start pumping fluids from our enclosed tanks to sea. Even though the hull creaked under the sea pressure as rivets popped, we could still force fluids out. The whirl of the pumps ejecting fluids made me start to relax a little. Now it was a matter of time until we got rid of the extra weight and began rising to the surface. But, would we run out of air first?

Hour after hour passed and I got very cold as moisture started to run down the inside walls. I sat down on the deck beside the helm putting my arms around my legs trying to stay warm at the cold depths.

"No unnecessary talking or moving to conserve oxygen," the

captain ordered. After a while the ship's corpsman, our doctor, went and broke open a glass tube in each compartment to measure the carbon monoxide. He had to move some people to a different compartment as their compartment air became polluted.

The cold spread up my arms so I curled up in the fetal position to stay as warm as I could. The hours passed slowly—fourteen, fifteen, and sixteen and then seventeen hours—I waited, hoping and praying in the cold gray light.

Suddenly, I heard a terrifying sound of creaking metal and wondered if we were starting to break apart. I felt movement as the submarine started to slowly roll upright from its right side. A loud metallic grinding and popping sound echoed throughout the boat, as the bow scraped against the ocean's rocky bottom. I looked up from inside my metal coffin at the ceiling thinking, "Has God granted me more time, or will we roll down into deeper water and be crushed?"

We had less than an hour's worth of air left as we huddled on the jagged rocky bottom listening to the hull pop and clang. We knew at any moment the hull could burst, and we would spend eternity in a twisted metal grave. The popping sounds slowed as we lifted out of the depths, breaking free of the bottom. We slowly rose and erupted out through the surface, with the sea waves crashing evenly across the deck. We had no air left in our pressure tanks to blow the remaining water out of our tanks. The enginemen started the low pressure air pump and slowly the deck rose up out of the sea.

Our senior after torpedo room man, Dick Sweeney, and the damage control party went onto the after deck and checked the damage. Just ten feet from where I stood a ship had crashed into us and the V of its hull had gone up over my head and cut off a mast. The ship rammed down the teak deck, tearing and crushing the after trim tank, ripping off the capstan and stern light.

A main engine was started, the propellers started to turn and our boat shook violently. The captain yelled, "All stop!" A diver was sent over the rear deck and found the propellers and rudders were badly dented. Our radio mast was ripped off so we couldn't call for help, either. The submarine shook as our one bent propeller drove us forward with the decks still awash. Somehow the rivets and hull had withstood the pressure well beyond our crush depth.

A destroyer communicated to us by light that a supertanker, the Export Adventurer, with Captain Roger Kidd in command, had rammed us by accident. Later we learned the tanker had wandered into our Military Area and almost hit the destroyer. The sound of the destroyer's high pitched propellers had masked out the sound of the tanker, which is why we couldn't hear them. The inexperienced reserve destroyer crew didn't warn us on the UQC, our underwater telephone.

I learned later that the chief petty officer from the destroyer, aboard as an observer, had wet his pants as he stood terrified in the middle of our ward room isle.

The supertanker was over two football fields long, seventy-five feet wide and its keel was over a hundred feet deep. Our sub was at periscope depth, just sixty-five feet down. The captain's quick action of making the bow rise and lowering the after deck saved us from certain death. This upwards angle let the supertanker slide down along the after deck and prevented us from being cut in half, both parts dropping separately to the ocean floor, killing all of us.

The destroyer escorted us back to the submarine base in New London. I saw the high command was waiting for us on the dock, with the gold on their uniforms shining in the sun. We were not allowed to leave the boat as our officers were escorted to the upper base for debriefing. Over the next couple of days, each one of us involved in the collision were brought to a military inquiry court to testify. The military recording clerk spoke into a microphone, rubber mask over his mouth, and quoted verbatim each word I spoke.

My fellow electricians told me the engineering officer had tried to get the signed speed log from the maneuvering room controller man. Instead he received a copy. The speed log is our Bible, a signed document of all the speed changes during the event. It could be altered to put the blame elsewhere, changing someone else's career.

After several weeks we heard the verdict: the captain was found guilty of negligence. The Exsport Adventurer, commanded by Captain Kidd, had wandered into our military area. The destroyer that was manned by reserve sailors didn't call us, but it did not matter.

Our captain, Lieutenant Commander William Evans, was transferred to shore duty in Green Bay, Alaska. We had a huge ship going away party for him. His actions had saved our lives. We presented him with a fur-lined jockstrap for his new ice cold Alaskan assignment.

The Captain is Always Responsible for His Ship!!

CHAPTER 8

World War II Surprise

Submarine Next To Pier

I was the leading seaman in charge of the deck gang aboard the submarine, Angler. My group had to maintain and paint everything outside the hull, and provide guard duty in port. At sea, we stood all the outside watches no matter what the weather.

In port when a guard is relieved from duty, he disconnects his pistol belt and passes it to the oncoming watchman. The new guard puts on the belt, and checks the .45 caliber pistol to make sure it is unloaded. This was repeated seven times a day, seven days a week, month after month without a problem.

One warm evening in New London, Connecticut, the topside watch was changing guard. The oncoming sailor dropped one end of the pistol belt. To his horror, the .45 caliber pistol and holster slid off the opposite end and over the ship's side. I was called and had to inform the captain of this major event! In the morning, our submarine base divers were called to recover the weapon. They arrived at first light, and tied up their diving barge to our submarine. I showed them about where I thought the weapon had gone over the side. Putting on their tanks, they dove down into the murky water and searched for a while.

One diver surfaced beside our submarine and said to me, "I have good news and I have bad news." The good news, I found the .45, but the bad news is a World War Two Torpedo is buried in the mud right under the boat."

The entire submarine base had to be evacuated to retrieve the torpedo! All diesel and nuclear submarines backed out from their peers, and went out to sea.

The rusted old torpedo was carefully lifted out of the mud, and placed on a barge to be detonated later. Fortunately, it didn't explode while being jiggled and twisted out of the river bottom!

It was a stroke of good luck that this time bomb was found. During hurricanes, all submarines in port, lengthened their mooring lines, and submerged right next to their pier. In the previous twenty plus years of hurricanes, submarines had submerged right on top of it many times. The submarine ballast tanks bottoms are opened to the sea, making them vulnerable from underneath. The submarines are moored only twenty feet apart, and if one blew up it would probably start a chain reaction.

Most people think that the safety mechanism on a nuclear missile would stop a nuclear explosion. While this is true, each submarine on the thirty-six piers had sixteen torpedoes, and enough fuel to travel six thousand miles. That is over seven hundred torpedoes with 550 pounds of high explosives each— or, *three hundred and eighty-five thousand pounds* of high explosives, plus over fifty nuclear missiles, and three nuclear reactors with millions of gallons of fuel. This would make one hell of a Molotov cocktail! This fire ball of radioactive particles from broken containers would be thrown into the air. New London, Connecticut is less than a mile away, and just a few miles distance across the bay from Long Island, New York. The Gulf Stream is around the edge of Rhode Island, not far away is Boston, Massachusetts just a couple hundred miles away upwind.

The ship hulls on our submarines are less than an inch thick, and are not built to withstand that type of explosion. I think of it today, just how close we all were to death any stormy day. We were laughing and enjoying steak and coffee, watching movies in the Hurricane, while sitting on top of Armageddon.

CHAPTER 9

Thrown Overboard

Submariners are a small volunteer force, less than one percent of the Navy. We received "hazardous duty" pay, which combined with our regular pay came to three dollars a day in 1960.

My assignment on board was to learn every system. It didn't matter what your profession was; a cook, electrician, or engine man—everyone had to fire a torpedo, cook a meal, or put in a battery charge. After learning each system, high pressure air, hydraulic, water, fuel etc., I was tested by a certified enlisted man in that field. Then, the officer in charge of that specialty tested me the final time.

After nine months of training, I was ready for an overall final test on everything. It started after the evening meal, in port with the lieutenant commander training officer. He walked me through the boat, identifying items and proposed complex problems to solve on every system from memory; no time to check a book. "Seconds mean life or death in any real crisis." Even though I was an electrician, he had me start an engine, prepare to fire a torpedo, and answer questions about cross-connecting systems to bypass damaged submarine sections. The testing continued through each compartment until three in the morning.

Physically and mentally exhausted after nine hours of testing, I officially became a submariner. This event let me wear silver dolphins, unlike a pilot's wings. I had to be able to perform anyone's job.

Officers trained for a year in school and at sea to get their gold dolphins. The feeling of relief and sense of pride swelled within me, I was now part of an elite group, and accepted into the brotherhood by my fellow submariners.

Officers being trained were taken out regularly to perform battle strategies, and fire dummy torpedoes at real targets in mock battles at sea. They learned what to listen for on sonar, and how to identify targets, plus how much to lead targets at different distances in all types of weather and hit the target. Some would be in the ward room looking at all the incoming info to plan a course to intercept, or figure out multiple targets and what they were up to. At the *tbt* computer analyzer in the conning tower, the new officers cranked in distance and angle on the bow information from sightings through the periscope. The total information from all tactical centers received, set up the final path before firing a torpedo. After firing, they watched the watch second hand, and fired up to three torpedoes. Each time we fired, the nose of the submarine rose like a rifle recoil, and we waited till the sub settled down before firing again. Firing three in succession would stop the 2400 ton submarine right in place. Each is fired with high pressure air out the twenty-four-foot-long tube, and then the torpedo propellers spin at high speed till impact. There is a small wheel that spins on its side, arming the torpedo at a safe distance. Other torpedoes have a homing device in their nose, and the attached information cable is cut off by a knife at the end of the torpedo tube. They arm at a distance, and go for the loudest target.

In port, a new man on board was lying on his bed watching a movie that I was showing. I saw him spinning that little wheel when the lights went on for me to change a movie reel. All hell suddenly broke loose; we now had a fully armed torpedo among eleven other torpedoes loaded with high explosives. The submarine had to be evacuated, and neighboring subs had to move out and away. If the front of the torpedo was bumped, it could trigger an explosion, so it had to be off loaded live. Volunteer torpedo men went back aboard to undertake this very dangerous unloading.

Six men in the torpedo room used chain falls to move the one ton plus weapon. It had to be shifted to the middle of the torpedo room, and pulled back onto a loading skid. Four chain falls connected to the skid corners raised it, until the skid's rear end was lifted to a thirty-degree up angle. Then, they aligned it with our small torpedo hatch to be retrieved back out the hatch. A special padded metal basket was placed over the torpedo nose, and two ropes were attached to it and passed to us. The deck skid was flipped over for me, and another to carefully raise it up. First, I attached my rope end to the hydraulic capstan and put three turns around it, and signaled to turn it on. The other deck hand pulled in the slack on his side till it wedged. Then, I locked my line onto the deck cleat, and he moved his line to the capstan and started the same. We could move it but twelve inches at a time, moving and locking our lines till it lay on the deck skid. A four-wheel torpedo loader with a long arm rode over the pier, and aligned beside the torpedo. The arm carefully moved over the torpedo, my nerves were getting very tight. A misstep would take us all. A metal band was slipped under the weapon's middle, and lines were attached to each end. The operator slowly raised the torpedo, and we aligned it to the waiting skid on the side of the loader. All lines were removed and the loader crept and moaned on the wooden boards down the pier, where a man with a red flag walked far in front.

Yes, torpedoes do malfunction, and homing ones are our worst nightmare.

Once, we fired one and it armed right away. We were the loud-est target, and it turned back to ram us. We had to dive and surface to get away till its battery ran out of power. I felt fear as I listened to the buzzing sound passing by outside the hull from different directions over and over.

The black crystal on the front of some torpedoes was so sensi-tive, that I had to wear gloves up to my armpits when loading them to prevent damage. The heat from my hand would ruin its capability of picking up the heat of a match at a quarter of a mile.

The battle training was for the officers to learn how to compen-sate for the many variables, because the closer the submarine is to land the more fresh water in the sea or currents made the torpedo react differently. The torpedo is guided by two internal gyros, that set the upper and lower limits of travel. This allows it to ignore one target to get a better one. Destroyers run a shallow draft, and an aircraft carrier goes down over a hun-dred feet; the gyros prevent the shallow targets from blocking a main target.

In war games, we fire a torpedo that will pass ten feet under the target's bottom, and travel out to a total of five miles. Instead of high explosives in the nose, it's filled with five-hundred and fifty pounds of fresh water. The fresh water is automatically expelled after its travel, and it floats vertically. After firing the torpedo, we surface and travel on the fired path. The lookouts look for the fluorescent nose of the 18-23 foot weapon, and we retrieve it. The submarine eight-man retrieval crew was on deck with a diver with two safety handlers. Six men rigged the rope through the pulley, and lowered the hook to be attached by the diver.

On this particular day, our submarine had fired a torpedo and the unexpected happened! The diver jumped into the ocean with his safety ropes held by his two handlers. He slid a large metal band around the torpedo to the middle balance point, and attached the hook. Two other lines were attached, one to the front and I held the back one. We aligned the torpedo sideways with the rock and rolling submarine.

The diver gave the thumbs up sign, and six men started pulling the line to our power winch. The torpedo rose into the air, and we two handlers pulled on our lines to align it.

Suddenly there was a big swirl, and I saw a sixteen-foot shark ram the diver. His two safety men yanked him away so hard, they banged him against the sub, knocking him out. He hung in a limp arc, banging against the ship's metal side.

Onboard, men started arguing about shooting the shark that circled under the diver. This had never happened before, so there was no "shark watch." The submarine rose up and down in the waves, pitching from side to side as they dragged the unconscious diver up and across the deck. The torpedo started to sweep, stern first across the deck, forcing me off the opposite side.

I yelled, "watch the fish," the nickname of a torpedo. The person who held the front line was watching the shark, as he quickly yanked hard to pull in his line. The torpedo nose spun

Torpedo

in across the deck, and thrusted the torpedoes back out over the water. This caused my line to quickly lock tight on my hand, and pulled me over the side into the air down over the shark. I quickly frogged, a trick my father taught me while I was very young growing up out in the country.

My Dad showed me how to spring out my hands and feet in opposite directions. This prevents you from hitting your head, while falling to the ground or plunging too deep, if falling into any water.

Luckily, my left fingertips caught the torpedo's center rope. This spun me around, letting me slide down the rope onto the torpedo. I locked both arms and feet in a death grip, around the twenty-three foot long greased weapon. I was past the balance point and its nose started to rise up, as I slowly slid down toward the waiting circling shark just inches below my feet. I screamed at the top of my lungs, "get me on deck, get me on deck!" The upward angled torpedo was raised quickly with me still piggybacked on it. They pulled me up across the teak deck, and dropped me down still sandwiched to the torpedo. I was able to pull my arms and legs out just in time to avoid being crushed under the torpedo.

The dazed diver and I lay side-by-side on the deck, totally exhausted, breathing heavily. Looking at each other, our eyes said what our mouths couldn't.

What a hell of a story to tell our grandchildren!

CHAPTER 10

Training Junior Officers

We trained a dozen submarine school officers simultaneously on the hunter killer submarine Angler. They learned all the special tactics of war, from standing watch topside, sighting targets, and determining their direction of travel and speed during the day or night. When we were submerged, the deck officer became the diving officer. Each student had to dive the boat, and quickly get our submarine trimmed and balanced.

The USS Angler was cruising along on a warm summer afternoon in Long Island. I was the starboard lookout, leaning back and enjoying the sun on my face. I heard someone call out, "permission to come up?" The deck officer said, "granted." The mess cook emerged through the hatch with a five-gallon bucket of table scraps. He looked around and said, "permission to go on deck and dump garbage." The deck officer said, "ok, but be carefull." The mess cook went down the two steps in front of me, and opened the small side door leading to the deck. I leaned over the side to watch him struggle with the heavy bucket, along the narrow deck beside our sail. When he got to the after deck, he clipped on the rope to the bucket handle, and wrapped the other end around his hand. Leaning over the side, he tipped the bucket of food and shook it. Before I could yell

Nooo… he turned the bucket with the opening down, and to my horror threw it into the sea. He was abruptly yanked over the side and disappeared. I yelled "man overboard starboard side aft." The officer screamed into the deck microphone "man over board starboard side, stop the rotation of the starboard screw." He yelled down through the hatch "right full rudder." Back at the power cubicle, the Electrician slowed the engine, and threw the lever for the right propeller into neutral, then reverse, and back into neutral. This action prevented the mess cook from being sucked into the props. I kept my eyes on the mess cook, and could only see his head bob up and down between the waves, as we moved further and further away. The officer said "where away." I pointed at my target, but soon had to use my binoculars to find him. We made a wide arch hundreds of yards away from him, all the time, I kept my arm pointing straight at him. If I looked away, I would loose sight of him in a second, and never find him again among the waves. We slowed down and reversed direction, and edged toward him slowly. He was just a dot now, and the officer pulled the 310-foot sub up to him. The sailors on deck threw him a rope, and he coiled it around his arm and held tight. They dragged him to the turtle back at the rear of the boat. The rescue crew pulled him out of the water, and saw the rope still held tight in the other hand. The shaking and terrified sailor was helped to the after battery hatch, and sent below. His inexperience lead him to throw the bucket face first, instead of bottom first. Throwing the bucket face first created a sea anchor, which pulled him overboard. When it is thrown bottom first, a little water is splashed into the long stainless steel tube, and it's swished around and dumped. He was very lucky it was summer and all went well, In winter time, you have two minutes before the cold locks you up, and then you sink. I was told that if I fell over in the winter to make peace with my GOD, because they couldn't turn around in time.

Living with these student officers was difficult, because of the many life threatening mistakes they made. After training many groups, I learned the officer's routine, and attempted to prepare myself before their mistakes became a crisis for me. However, I didn't always see a mistake coming, and it almost cost me my life.

One cold and windy night in heavy seas, I stood lookout with the storm's impact of high waves crashing down on me. I wore three coats; a pair of wool gloves inside leather mittens plus heavy fur lined canvas pants. Around my middle was a six-inch-wide canvas belt with four inch leather belt attached on top. Hanging from the leather belt were three chains, two forward and one aft. I connected the chains to the sub to prevent me from being washed over the side.

I scanned the horizon for any target lights among the waves. A contact could easily be missed by the ship's radar, because we constantly were bobbing up and down. Targets are not always up on top of a wave at the same time that we were, and it takes fourteen seconds for the radar to rotate completely around. They would have to be on the top of the wave, at the same time as our radar unit was pointing in their direction.

Each time the waves crashed down on top of me, I held my breath till the ocean receded below my mouth. Lookouts rotated every half-hour to the conning tower below to warm up. It didn't take long before I could hardly move my limbs, and became cold and stiff from the windswept waves and ice forming all over me.

On this very cold night, a junior officer stood watch huddled under his fiberglass bubble staring into the storm's fury. He stepped out from under his bubble to speak to me over the loud ocean roar.

Suddenly, the loud diving alarm sounded aooga, in the crisp air and throughout the submarine below! The startled officer turned forward to see what was happening, and then turned back toward me with a blank, scared look. Another loud aooga sounded in the howling wind, two-aooga sounds mean emergency crash dive, as fast as you can.

Immediately, all the main ballast tank vents opened with a loud booming sound. The escaping air sprayed water up into the air in front of me, like a pod of whales sounding. There was no time to explain, the submarine was diving below the waves!

I struggled to disconnect my chains with my ice-coated gloves. In less than thirty seconds, the submarine would be below the waves. I scrambled and jumped down through the top hatch, turned and dropped through the second hatch down onto the control room floor. The officer jumped down last, as water began pouring in through the open hatch. He fell sprawling on the conning tower floor, and quickly leaped up through the incoming water and grabbed the hatch cord handle. He fell off the ladder backwards, slamming it shut. The quarter master leaped up through the incoming water, and spun the handle sealing the hatch. Below, I turned the diving plane wheel to full dive, and we continued down to sixty-five feet, our periscope depth.

The captain came running into the control room to see what the emergency was. He wondered if we were going to be hit or ram into something. When the diving horn makes that aooga sound twice, it could mean an imminent collision with a ship, torpedo, or inbound missile.

The junior officer explained to the captain, that his sleeve flap had caught on the diving handle when he turned to speak to me!

That was a very close call; in another *ten seconds* the craft would have flooded through the open hatch bringing us all to the bottom.

The red-faced young officer was relieved from duty, and the captain took the still ice-coated man to his cabin for a little "TALK!"

CHAPTER 11

North and South Pier Two

While on a three-week mission on the submarine *Angler* in New York Long Island Sound, we were training a dozen new submarine officers in sub war tactics. Their final learning event was to drive the submarine up the Thames River, and moor it at our New London, Connecticut submarine base. A student junior officer was to moor the sub next to a pier, an extremely difficult job. All of the piers are angled at 45°, facing up river. This made it faster for subs to back out and escape in emergencies, but more difficult to return and tie up. A submarine had to fight the current up river then stop and pivot. Each propeller is pushing in opposite directions turning the submarine toward the pier opening. When the 310-foot submarine is aligned, we shoot ahead alongside a pier and tie up. The main problem is that when the bow gets in between the piers, there is no current pushing sideways on the bow, but heavy current pushing on the stern. The pivoting action on the boat requires extra power and maneuvering to stay aligned. Since there are no brakes, timing has to be just right, or we will rush forward and crash into the pier or into another boat.

The ship-yard workers came out of their shops with their coffee cups, ready to be entertained by a mooring show. They had nicknamed the *Angler* "the Mangler", because of the many times we had crashed into the pier. Routinely, we wrecked many of the bow's 58-vertical sonar tubes, while training the inexperienced students.

First Lieutenant Burke was standing at attention on the bow with his three-man anchor crew. Other crew members stood on deck by the other three mooring lines, ready to attach to the pier. The captain watched the junior officer give orders to start his approach to the pier. The ship shuddered all over, as the sub began turning in the heavy current. The student officer kept adding more and more power, but the sub's stern continued to be swept down-river. He passed our assigned pier at the wrong angle, and had to abort the landing. He ordered the helmsman to turn the sub back down-river to restart his approach again, all the while the captain kept barking orders in his ears. Now, the officer circled around to the end of the line with the other submarines. Their other junior officers also were headed upstream, waiting to try their landing. Each boat had to maintain their place in line, while not interfering with the one ahead or behind them. A submarine is two-thirds submerged in the nine-knot river current, and it takes power and timing to maneuver correctly into the narrow slot between another moored sub and his space. This time the student officer went in at ramming speed, and ordered the rudder moved in the wrong direction! The boat leaned over abruptly and turned, smashing right through the heavy duty ten-foot wide wooden pier! Lieutenant Burke was tossed over the boat's side, and laid flat on the pier with everyone on deck knocked down. Several thirty-foot long pier supports sky rocketed at weird angles up into the air, and bounced across the deck landing like a pile of pick-up sticks. Fortunately, no one got hit from the pilings rolling along the deck.

The captain yelled, "Get back on deck!" to the still-groggy lieutenant as he staggered down the pier. He was trying to find a spot on the deck even enough to jump back onboard from the pier. The sub was wedged solidly into the pier to the delight of the laughing shipyard workers. We made another mundane day very exciting for them again. The sonar men worked through the night replacing many of the eight-foot long sonar tubes.

The radio man sent a message to base operations, "USS *Angler* moored north AND south pier two." The captain did not see the humor in it at all, and demoted the radio man one pay grade. However, the crew thought it was hilarious to see an officer sprawled on the pier in his dress uniform.

There were always comical mooring stories of training students bouncing off or ramming into other subs or piers, after all, they were just learning!

I remember watching the submarine *Becuna* returning from a Navy yard retrofit with a brand new multimillion-dollar sonar dome mounted on the front bow. It had taken four months to add this high tech detection gear in the Philadelphia Navy yard. The main power controller man made a wrong move, when the propellers were reversed to stop the sub and prevent the engines from tripping out by over speeding. That's like putting your car in neutral at sixty-miles per hour. The deafening sound of the bow being crushed up against the pier made everyone close their eyes, turn away, and wince. It was now just broken scrap metal—a very expensive one at that!

My favorite story that was ever heard made our mistake seem trivial. This tale was about a submarine that came in, commanded by a very nervous junior officer who used too much power. As his submarine turned quickly in the heavy current, he ordered too much power. The engines raced faster and faster, as he tried to recover from his mistake. The propellers were frothing up the water, as the sub rammed into and slid along the side of the pier. The front of the 2,400-ton vessel crashed up and over the front retaining wall. The bow was thrust up onto the road, and slid twenty-five feet into the parking area hitting a telephone booth. The telephone booth was torn out of the ground, and thrown through the windshield of the captain's car.

I pity the captain after filling out his car insurance accident report. I can imagine the insurance adjuster asking him, "You state here that your car windshield was broken by someone driving a submarine, which crashed into a telephone booth, throwing it through the front windshield of your car?"

The true stories are better than anything you could possibly imagine!

CHAPTER 12

Red Light—Green Light

One mission sent the *Submarine Angler* north on an inland sea route, an easy trip through the Cape Cod Channel. We would pass through the tip of Massachusetts on our way up to the windswept icy cold North Atlantic waters.

Our submarine waited south of the Cape Cod Channel for a pilot to guide us through its winding narrow path. The channel is just a couple hundred yards wide; therefore, large ships must be accompanied as they carefully navigate through. A plugged channel would force ships to go out around Cape Cod, adding many hours to a trip. I spotted a small red boat bobbing through the waves with the word PILOT written in big white letters on its side. The boat arrived and the pilot was brought to the bridge to meet with our captain.

I was the port, left-side lookout, enjoying the ride through the channel on this warm breezy night. We traveled up through the channel, approaching the Sagamore Bridge. I looked up to watch the cars ride across it. White lights glowed, like a string of Christmas lights, all across the underside of the bridge—white light after white light. A green light, then white lights again, and a red light.

All of a sudden, it dawned on me that there shouldn't be any colored lights on the underside of the bridge. I knew what this meant and immediately yelled out, "*Ship dead ahead, collision course!*"

I pointed out the colored lights on the bridge span, and the lieutenant rang the collision alarm. The pilot and deck officer Lieutenant Burke stared ahead, but couldn't see any ship. The sound echoed through the sub, and the crew sprang into action locking all hatches. Then, we spotted it—a high, multi-tiered, deep-sea fishing trawler. We were black and much lower than the fishing vessel, making it hard for them to distinguish us in low light.

Our sub had no place to go, and there was not enough room for two large ships to pass by each other in the narrow channel. We blew our ship's whistle over and over and moved to our right, expecting to run aground. The charts indicated it was way too shallow for us to stay afloat. Mud started to be kicked up into the air by our two huge six foot high propellers. People ran out of their homes along the banks of the canal and stood on their lawns, watching the two enormous ships race at each other. If we slowed, we would sink into the mud instead of surfing through the pudding mass.

I could see men on the trawler hanging over the side staring down at me, as we passed under the curvature of their hull. I was trapped in my metal lookout hole with nowhere to run, looking up at the trawler's v-shaped hull, hundreds of yards of steel passing by, just a few feet from my head. Our phone talker went running back down the deck ripping the phone headset off. He joined the bow lookout, both now posed in a diving position on the opposite side, ready to dive into the mud and water mix when we made contact. I saw civilians holding their hands over their mouths, wide-eyed in disbelief less than a hundred yards away. I turned my head into my shoulder, and closed my eyes and waited for impact. Like driving past a billboard on a super highway, we flew by each other.

In a flash it was over, the sound of our ship's whistle still echoing in my ears, as it bounced off their hull and the surrounding houses. We had somehow passed by each other without making contact!

People were standing on their lawns cheering in relief, but they couldn't see my shaking knees or my body trembling with fear.

The control center had told us a small fishing boat was coming the other way, but we learned that was not the case. The channel control center had made a terrible error, sending two large ships jousting at each other. My chance sighting of the colored lights stopped a major Cape Cod collision from appearing on every TV news broadcast that evening. I could envision helicopters circling over the two-tangled ships, with cameras zooming in on me in my crushed lookout hole.

The cars on the bridge had a ringside seat for all this action. I hope none of the rubbernecked spectators had their own collision watching the landlocked sea battle.

CHAPTER 13

Russians at the Statue

Manhattan Sky Line Straight Ahead

There was little time for me to relax on board our WW II Hunter Killer Submarine. This time the crew would not be launching frogmen, while submerged laying mines or photographing Russian ships. We would have a relaxing summer weekend giving tours of our submarine, at least, that's what I thought. In 1962, the submarine Angler, was sent to the New York City Harbor front on a good-will tour. It was a clear sunny day as we backed out from our berth in New London, Connecticut. After going under the Gold Star Memorial Bridge, we turned and soon cleared by Race Rock Island, and turned out into Long Island Sound. Everyone aboard was excited to have a fun-filled weekend in Manhattan.

Finally, an assignment in which we did not have to creep in on patrol, just a well-deserved vacation. I would have time off to see the sun, visit, drink, and meet women, not necessarily in that order. We entered New York's inner harbor, and I poked my head out of the after torpedo room hatch. I could see Manhattan spread out before me with its magnificent sky line. I jumped up on the deck and snapped a picture as the submarine turned, poised between two tall buildings. Down below me, the speakers bellowed, "Man the maneuvering watch, man the maneuvering watch." Free time over, I left to be the port lookout.

I was one of several crew members that had special jobs when entering port. On the forward deck stood one group; an officer, phone talker and line handlers, and the other group was all the way aft with a phone talker and line handlers. I stood on the bridge with an officer and another lookout. As the port lookout, my job was to scan the horizon on the left side for obstacles in the water or small pleasure boats. The other lookout did the same on the right side. The radar only picks up large objects above the waves, so any logs or small debris bobbing up cannot be detected.

I was checking out the girls at the Statue of Liberty through my binoculars, like I was supposed to be doing? Then, I turned to my left and saw something sticking up out of the water. It was a Russian periscope. I blinked my eyes in disbelief, but there it was square and black and looking back at me. Our periscopes are gray and oval; yes, this was definitely a Russian submarine.

I called out, "Russian periscope bearing ten degrees off the port bow." The deck officer said, "Don't fool around like that, Ski."

"I'm not fooling, Sir!"

"What," exclaimed the officer. He quickly turned the powerful deck—mounted binoculars onto the target. The officer screamed into the deck microphone, "Captain to the bridge"!

The urgency in his voice brought our captain, Commander William Evans, rushing to the bridge. The deck officer reported to the captain, who then searched with his binoculars for the Russian periscope. It popped up and the captain yelled to the radioman below, "Send to New London, Russian submarine my position, New York Inner Harbor, advise?"

We stopped, and the Russian scope dropped beneath the waves. To our right was Wall Street, and Manhattan just a half mile away; on the left was the Statue of Liberty less than the length of a couple of football fields.

The bong, bong, bong of the battle alarm rang throughout the boat below. The captain said over his microphone, "This is not a drill, this is not a drill." The crew started arming torpedoes, activating battle screens, and locking their compartment hatches shut. Each compartment was now contained; if one area became punctured the rest of us would still survive. All compartments have a phone talker, who reports to the bridge. The bridge phone talker reported to the captain, "All compartments manned and ready."

I strained my eyes, peering through the binoculars, I could make out the faint shape of the Russian submarine beneath the waves. The Russian was hiding in sixty feet of water, and it takes fifty feet of water to cover him. I could see the flattened out waves over its shape like a rock in a shallow stream. Twenty minutes passed and New London called us back, "Sleepy Hollow (our code name), chase her out of there!"

Our submarine turned and pointed all our now-armed torpedoes straight at the Russian submarine.

Suddenly, a second Russian submarine splashed up into the air near the first. Her two missiles on the front deck gleamed in the sun as she sunk back beneath the waves. The second submarine must have tried to move, and bounced off the shallow muddy bottom. The captain again called New London, and reported there were two Russian submarines. In a few minutes, the message came back, "Chase the two of them out of there!"

Our three sixteen-cylinder engines roared into action ready for battle! I could see the fish-shaped silhouettes of both clearly now. Our submarine zigged back and forth staying between the Russian submarines and Manhattan. At their distance, a fired torpedo would take less than a half a minute to take out most of the Manhattan area. If the weapons were nuclear-tipped, they would obliterate all of New York City, the financial heart of the United States.

Thirty to forty-five minutes went by, as we forced the two Russian warriors out and away into deeper water. The sonar man heard the whining sound of a nuclear submarine. This sound comes from their reactor's steam turbine, making it easy to identify. The captain yelled to the sonarman below, "Send a message on Gertrude, our underwater telephone, Unknown Nuki, (their nick name), this is Sleepy Hollow, Identify?" This was done several times, but no reply! The captain had New London called, and asked "What nuclear submarine did you send to help us with the Russians?" Approximately thirty minutes went by and our answer came back, "All of ours are accounted for, *Ram Him!*"

Five more American submarines were sent to hunt with us, and quickly surrounded the Russian nuclear submarine. Three submarines circled around him from above and the other three submerged to circle around him. One by one each submarine charged straight at the Russian sub but each time he dodged them. Like a matador at a bull fight, he turned quicker than we could. We kept trying to damage the Russian rudder or diving planes, and force him to surface. Then, the United States would have all their latest technology to study and reverse engineer.

The hours clicked by, and it became much harder to manipulate in the dark. One wrong turn and the Russian would be gone, either completing her mission or escaping.

We didn't know if the **prey** would become the **hunter,** and fire one of her many missiles into New York City. Three days of bull fighting around the clock had moved our submarines far down off the Virginia Coast line. Here in very deep water, we were spread out further apart. Each submarine sonarman listened intently for any sign of movement on their part or on our part. The slightest giveaway like in a poker game, and the game was lost. The pressure built as nerves tightened, I could visualize the same response on the Russian sub with all ears straining to hear any movement, so they could out flank us. I'm sure the Russian sub was afraid of being captured, and their true mission exposed.

How quickly things changed. One of our subs lunged, and the Russian "shark" dodged the incoming submarine. Then, the Russian submarine quickly shot out, and sped away gaining her freedom. The Russian submarine dropped down into the canyon-filled depths below at full power, and in a flash disappeared. There was no way any of us could ever find or catch them in the mountain high peaks and canyon maze below us.

Exhausted, we surfaced and together retreated back to our different bases to wait for another cold-war mission. One mistake by either side could have started a nuclear holocaust.

Why were three Russian submarines in New York inner harbor with dozens of torpedoes and missiles? Why were these Russian submarines only eight, football-field lengths away from Manhattan and Wall Street?

This happened in the spring just before the Cuban Missile Crisis.

Recently, I was watching a documentary, which showed during the Cuban Missile Crisis, that there were four undetected Russian-diesel submarines hiding between Florida and Cuba with nuclear-tipped torpedoes. It was not until 2006, that one of the Russian submarine captains revealed this secret. During the Cuban Crisis, the only information the Russian subs could receive was from our radio stations. They were out of touch with their command for three weeks, only hearing about our troop buildup in Florida getting ready to invade Cuba. They were unsure if we were at war. One submarine captain and an executive officer both had their keys in the nuclear control panel turned and ready to fire. The submarine group commander refused permission for that captain to fire his nuclear-tipped torpedo. The documentary said, that when the four submarines returned to Russia, they were perceived as cowards.

By accident, did I stop something from happening a year before the Cuban Missile Crisis?

Only GOD knows for sure.

CHAPTER 14

No Respect for the Admiral

Saluting the Colors

The command of our submarine base changes every few years, and this year was one of them. Thousands of officers and sailors from the base schools plus submarine squadrons two, four, six, eight, and ten, prepared for the intense inspection of themselves, and their submarines by Admiral Rickover. The admiral had a "no mercy" reputation, and would walk right up and look directly into your eyes. The fear and respect this man demanded was second only to God. He was the "Father of the Nuclear Navy," and King of the entire Submarine Force.

Day after day, we cleaned and painted from early morning to evening. The Submarines were spit shined inside, and freshly painted outside. We were inspected by our section chief, division officer, captain, and squadron commander. Everything had to be perfect for the Supreme Commander, Admiral Rickover. The day of command change finally came, and six thousand military personal converged into a gigantic field. The band sounds boomed out over the crowd. Thousands of sailors marching looked like a flock of white chickens warbling on their sea legs. Sailors don't march well, being used to the ocean rocking under our feet.

The entire submarine base personnel was gathered together for our first glimpse of the supreme commander. He stood with hat and coat covered in gold braid, his chest was full of medals, strutting like a South American dictator. After several hours of pomp and circumstance in the hot sun, we were dismissed to return to our submarines. Every type of submarine filled the lower base thirty-six piers, diesel hunter killers, fast attack, experimental, plus nuclear fast attack, and missile-firing boats. Their crews stood at attention in full dress white uniforms.

A sea of gold braid and medals flowed down to the lower submarine base to inspect. One by one, the admiral started aboard each submarine; stopped and saluted each ship's colors, the American Flag. The Bosun's whistle sounded, piping him aboard. "Comsublant arriving," blared over each submarine speaker, which was the admiral's official title. His title was Commander of all Submarines in the Atlantic.

Each submarine captain, when boarding, is called by his official title, submarine name, for example, "USS Angler arriving or leaving."

Our moment finally arrived, Admiral Rickover started across the gang plank, which was our entry way and he stopped halfway. He turned smartly, standing rigid at attention, and saluted our colors, the American flag. His white uniform embellished with a chest full of gold medals and rainbow-colored ribbons shone against our black submarine backdrop. He was a majestic, white-statuesque figure shining brightly in the afternoon sun. Neb, a salty, old WWII submarine sailor stood beside the brow, and blew the Bosun's whistle piping the admiral aboard.

This historic moment was challenged by a low flying sea gull, who thought to add to the occasion. The bird released a long wet bomb with deadly accuracy right on the admiral's hat. Then, the white-gray mass flowed slowly off the snow-white hat down one side, dropping onto all of the admiral's medals and gold buttoned dress white coat. The admiral never flinched, but stood at attention with his white gloved hand against his hat saluting.

When Neb stopped blowing the whistle, the admiral snapped his white gloved hand down by his side, pivoted in place and continued across the brow. He stepped down onto the submarine deck smartly. Neb standing at attention, with his medals and war patrol badges shining, stood beside him. Neb muttered out the side of his mouth," Aren't you glad elephants don't fly?"

The admiral burst into laughter and went down below into the submarine, still laughing and shaking his head. No more inspections for the entire fleet this day! After a while, the steward came up from below with the admiral's soiled uniform. It had to be cleaned, and pressed precisely to the admiral's critical specifications.

This sea gull showed the admiral no respect, but broke through his tough-guy image. The dirty bird saved us from many more hours of tension and torture in the red hot sun.

CHAPTER 15

Rough Sea Evacuation

Levers in Maneuvering Room

A submariner must pass many physical and physiological tests, designed to find any human frailty that would be stressed in our enclosed environment. Living in a narrow steel tube with barriers every twenty-five feet was the lifestyle I chose. Not seeing the sun for weeks on end, and smelling like my environment was similar to the existence of the galley slaves of old. Staying healthy was paramount to being a viable undersea warrior.

Our crew came from 125 different backgrounds, but became one family. We all lived together, and shared the same air. We traveled down the same two and a half foot wide corridor, seven days a week during our waking hours. There were no room for grudges or attitudes, as we were closer than family; our lives depended on each other.

On my submarine, I never had a cold or allergy attack, because of the lack of trees or mold in my environment. On our diesel submarine, if my sinuses or ears filled with fluid, they emptied abruptly when the sub snorkeled. Snorkeling occurs when we run an engine, while submerged by getting air through a three-foot wide pipe up to the surface. When a wave hit the top of this air intake pipe, the electrodes on top made the valve slam shut. The engine was still running, creating a vacuum throughout the boat. Any plugged sinuses or ears were quickly popped open out into the vacuum by the internal pressure in my body, like squeezing jelly out of a doughnut. When the wave cleared, the air valve opened and air returned, popping open my ears. I got used to this constant popping even in my sleep. If the vacuum level got too high, my tear ducts would squirt out fluid like a windshield washer. The engine safety trip-switch shuts down the engine, if six inches of vacuum is reached. We were not allowed to have any type of aerosol cans, deodorant, after-shave cans, or a bad tooth filling. Any pressure inside an item would explode in the vacuum.

I worked with a first class petty officer in charge of my electrical group. He was smart and in shape. He slept just two rows away from my bunk aboard ship, and we spoke about everything just like he was a big brother.

One night, he woke up screaming, holding his eyes in severe pain. I got the doctor, our corpsman, and he ran to check him out. We took my moaning friend out into the bright light of our mess hall. The Doc determined the tear ducts were sealed shut, causing his eyes to keep filling with fluid. A morphine injection was administered, but it was not enough to stop the pain, so he was given a second shot.

The captain was informed, and the submarine surfaced. The radio man called the base hospital, as we raced to get within a medical helicopter range.

Fluid kept building up in my friend's eyes, and he began screaming again. The morphine shots just took the edge off the pain, as he began rolling back and forth in his bunk holding his eyes. I wondered if we could get within range before his eyes ruptured.

We raced across and through oncoming waves, trying to get within the limits of the helicopter range. We traveled for half a day, before we received a radio call from the helicopter pilot trying to find us. We were just a black speck in the splashing waves and foaming sea below him. The captain turned on the flashing red light, and shot a red flare up into the air in the mid-day sun. The chopper still couldn't find us in all the wave action. Our lookout spotted the helicopter, but he only saw us after we fired another flare, and we gave him directions.

Now, the hard part was that the helicopter had to match all of the four ocean motions. The chopper began to lower, and to turn sideways to land across the narrow deck. Our submarine was going forward to slow down the sea's twisting actions. First, we rocked from side to side. Then second, the bow went up and down in the waves. Third, we dropped into the troughs between the waves, and rode up on the back of the last wave. Fourth, at any moment, the sea's action would pop us up toward the lowering helicopter. It took over an hour for the ace helicopter pilot to match all four movements.

The first class electrician was strapped into a basket stretcher, then passed vertically up through the middle hatch into incoming waves spraying down on us. A half dozen men on the deck lashed the basket onto the helicopter side, while fighting knee deep waves washing across the deck. He was flown to the submarine base hospital for emergency surgery. We crashed through the waves at standard speed, and arrived a day later. We learned the operation was a success, and he stayed in the hospital for a week, after which he returned to our sub to complete his recovery. We woke him every hour around the clock to put drops in his eyes. This prevented his tear ducts from resealing shut. He would plead with us to let him sleep, but we had to constantly wake him.

I was in an environment of pressure or vacuum with diesel fumes penetrating every fiber and pore of my body, twenty-four hours a day. We lived in this low-light world beneath the sea, away from the deafening running engines above, listening to our own heart beats in the stone-cold, quiet depths. At any time, it could be my turn, such as an appendix, kidney, or gall bladder attack. Bad accidents happen too. Would we be close enough for medical help? It is the risk that all submariners take, while operating alone and far away from land. Sometimes, we were unable to surface, because of our mission. We knew we were expendable for the good of the country, and we were all volunteers.

CHAPTER 16

Secret Missions

Torpedo Room Tubes

Hollywood has portrayed secret agents like 007, or Seal Teams as standing shoot-em ups. The Rambo-Dirty Harry type heroes never run out of bullets, or seldom get seriously hurt while fighting, and never miss a far-away shot. It is not the single or small group of "make my day types" that make things happen. When we submariners go on secret mission, I know "we are expendable." No one can come to rescue us. We can only survive, when we function as a team.

I was one of the hunter-killer, submarine crew of the USS Angler commanded by Captain William Evans, who volunteered for everything!

I recall one mission of the "we were never there type" that mimics a James Bond adventure. We all know that in real life "there are no do overs." Before our mission, we surrendered our dog tags and wallets, which were stored ashore, until or IF we returned.

This foggy morning our submarine travelled down the Thames River with secret, special guests. When we cleared the last bridge our hunter killer sub turned to head out into the open sea, hopefully undetected from the shore. Sometimes on look-out, I would see someone watching us through binoculars from the top of the surrounding high cliffs.

We submerged and quickly changed direction, and over the horizon we resurfaced. The sub rendezvoused with the diving barge, and divers drilled holes into our three thousand pound propellers. This changed the ship signature sound to prevent any recording from identifying or intercepting us on our return.

When we were far out at sea, the captain and executive officer opened the safe and took out our sealed orders. They signed a paper stating that the seal was unbroken on the package. These orders informed the captain the numbered chart to take out, and what multi-flat sided steering cam to use. Both of these units determined the real direction of travel for this mission. The executive officer pulled out the assigned numbered powder blue chart. The chart was half the size of a kitchen table with only numbers over it. No land, depth, or compass heading were indicated anywhere upon it. The steering cam was a six-inch plastic disk with many flat sides, that changed the steering compass true heading.

At battle stations, I stood on the other side of a clear wall and could see everything. My job was to gather information by headphone, and write it backwards on the wall for the attack team to see it. It showed a birds-eye view of what was happening above us. Our attack team would use this chart, and in the conning tower, the set of six-inch diameter numbered plastic cams for the mission. The cam was inserted behind the steering unit, and changed the actual heading indicated to what head quarters actually wanted for a direction of travel. The real numbers never showed. We traveled at the assigned depth for the given length of time and speed. After the assigned time, a new cam was inserted and a new direction was followed, and repeated until we arrived at the target area.

On this mission, we travelled submerged for three days. We only went near the surface to raise our snorkel air tube to pull in new air, and charge our 252 one-ton batteries. The engine exhaust mast is four feet below the surface of the water with a horse-shoe shaped top. This horse-shoe shaped top was filled with holes, which dispersed the smoke underwater leaving no trace to be spotted. When we started the engine, the back pressure created blew the water out of the three-foot diameter pipes, and we could then run the engine to charge our batteries.

Before the mission, the DRAI (Dead Reckoning Analyzer Indicator) window unit was taped over to prevent anyone from seeing our actual longitude and latitude. Normally, a reading is logged every half hour to track our non-secret trip course. Only the Mission Planners ashore knew where we went in order to maintain top security. If caught, none of the crew or frogmen had any information to tell the enemy.

After three days of twisting under the ocean, we arrived at our submerged destination.

The captain called through Gertrude, our underwater telephone, and announced "Sleepy Hollow on station!" We called our code name out every twenty minutes until we heard a reply. Out of the depths came another booming voice "steel bend on station." Two submarines were here, and soon we heard more subs call in by their code names until there were six submarines. None of us knew how many would be present on this operation. We all came undetected from different ports along the Atlantic seaboard.

The submarines edged closer together beneath the ocean to start the mission. Each submarine had twelve frogmen spread out through their compartments. This protected the frogmen if we were attacked; only the punctured compartment would lose those men.

The frogmen had no idea where they were, but only what to do once they swam away from each submarine. The order was given and all twelve frogmen moved to the forward torpedo room, and changed into their scuba gear. They were told: "don't pee in the trunk," but when the ice-cold Atlantic flooded up over their kidneys, it happened. The two frogmen flooded the escape chamber, till the pressure inside was the same as the outside. Then, they opened the hatch and swam out through the yellow-tinged water. They closed the door behind them, and the water was drained down into the subs bilge; it was depressurized for the next two to enter. When the pressure was equalized, the bottom hatch was opened for the next two. This action was repeated six times. The trunk was about one and a half times larger than a fifty-five gallon barrel. All the contaminated water was drained down, and then pumped back outside. The frogmen lined up on our deck, until all of the twelve-man team were out. When all six teams were ready, a signal was given, and the seventy-two frogmen swam away to execute their mission.

After a period of time, there was a clanking sound on the floor of the escape trunk; the frogmen had returned from their mission! They shut the outside trunk door, and we drained the trunk water inboard and depressurized it so they could reenter.

They lowered themselves down into our submarine dripping wet from their mission. The hatch was resealed and another team entered, clanked, and the process was repeated over and over till all were on board. The frogmen quickly got out of their gear, and dispersed throughout our many compartments.

I was an electrician in the maneuvering room, and manned the power cubicle that controlled the speed. I was conversing with a friendly frogman next to me, when orders came from the captain, "Get out of here at best possible speed." My assistant controller man and I started to pull and push the chrome speed levers in unison, through all five positions to series battery. This was the fastest that we could travel underwater. The submarine squatted down with the new-found surge of power, and sped off like a car at the INDY 500. A little power tweaking, and all 2400 tons were thrust through the ocean.

The high power running through the power cubicle made the resistors glow red, and created a humming sound with an ozone smell. All of a sudden, there was a huge explosion outside that lifted and shook our submarine. Unconsciously, I exclaimed aloud "What the hell was that?" The Frogman said nonchalantly, "Oh, there used to be an island there. It's now six-feet below sea level."

Eight-hundred men moved beneath the ocean undetected without any sign showing above us.

One-by-one, the submarines turned and travelled away in different directions on their preplanned secret routes. Unlike other branches of the military, medals are not awarded for bravery or for recognition: *"we were never there!"*

"Just another Non-Happening Event in the Silent Service."

CHAPTER 17

Hang On, and Lookouts Below

Months of standing just seven feet above the ocean gave me lots of time to think, co-existing with the many ocean moods that I endured. I was either trying to breathe in ice-filled ocean waves, or trying to breathe during terrifying hurricanes. Other times, hundreds of feet below the surface, we felt the raging energy crashing down from above. In the darkness of the depths, my life adjusted to the constant rocking or moaning sounds created by the storm action above.

We operated in Long Island Sound in spaces that were defined into fifteen by twenty-five mile wide blocks. Every day subs were traveling the same paths from our base, month after month for years. Just like cars that drove state and local highways, we knew little about what was around, above, or below us. It became routine after hundreds of trips to train submarine school students. I showed them how to dive, and control the football field long sub depth. Always watching the trainees and enduring many white-knuckled events, but none like the following story!

In the spring of 1961, the USS Angler SS240 prepared for routine training dives in Long Island Sound with sub-school students.

The officer on the bridge looked all about, and yelled to the two students, "Prepare to dive." His orders, "Dive, dive" echoed in the air! The ship's horn blared, "Aooga, aooga," and the two lookouts ducked out of their holes, and jumped down through the conning tower hatch. Turning, they would drop another ten feet to the control-room deck below.

They had only thirty-seconds before water started rushing into that hatch. The booming sound of the valves opening and water spraying up in the air in front of them, plus water rushing towards them could cause them to freeze in place. There is no stopping the sub and aborting the dive. Water still poured in through the hatch.

We trainers waited below to calm any fear the students might have. After rigging out the diving planes, they spun the diving wheels to "full dive." Our ever-watchful eyes made sure that any panic would be corrected instantly. The submarine pivoted and submerged into the depths. All around the students, other people were pulling tank-flooding levers, and the diving officer orders were shouted and answered. The angle of our submarine turned suddenly, passing the normal five degrees down angle. There was a feeling of helplessness, as the sub started to drop nose first faster and faster. I jumped on the bow-diving planes, and with the stern-diving planes man, we spun our wheels to full rise, before the deck acted as a wedge and we went vertical.

The diving officer yelled, "Blow negative and safety tank." We were still crash diving towards the bottom! He then screamed, "Blow all tanks, prepare for impact!" The needle on the shallow depth gauge slammed into the 250-foot maximum depth pin. Then the deep depth gauge started to spin, as we went deeper. Everyone braced for impact.

There are no brakes on a submarine; if the propellers were reversed the stern would be pulled upwards, making the sub more vertical. This would cause the deck to act as a ramming wedge forcing us down faster into the depths. The bow plowed into the bottom at 377 feet. The submarine shuddered as the stern crashed down, and the propellers dug into the sea bed. The sub layed on the bottom of Long Island Sound, water was pouring in around the now warped torpedo tubes. High pressure air was forced into the forward torpedo room, and the men held their ears and screamed to adjust to the high pressure air coming in, but HP Air is what stops the flooding. Fortunately, we rammed into a sandy bottom, and did not become entangled in some rocky bottom structure.

All main ballast tanks were blown free of water, and we all hoped we could break free of the bottom. The old World War II sub rocked to one side, and started to rise towards the surface. I thanked GOD that it was not built by the lowest bidder. Crushed and wounded, we started to ascend for what seemed like hours, but in reality was only minutes. She broke through the waves, and damage control parties checked their compartments. All reported to the captain, and only the torpedo room suffered damage.

The captain called the sub base to report the crash and asked for help. We slowly headed in towards our sub base; any speed would force more water into the torpedo room. After several hours, the lookouts spotted the floating dry dock ship sent to lift us up out of the sea. The ship towered above us, as they threw lines down to tie up to them. We locked their lines to our deck cleats, and aligned to the middle of its open bay. The multi-storied vessel has wide hollow sides with tanks inside, which they flood to sink below our keel. With their ropes attached to us, they pulled carefully and we slid into the behemoth's mouth. It took over an hour till our stern cleared, and they could close the opening behind us. Our sub was aligned to their sides in Gulliver type webbing, securing us solidly. The water was pumped out of their ship sides, and we slowly rose up out of the ocean. We were safe at last in the belly of the beast, and returned for repairs. The damage was extensive, warping the torpedo tubes and tearing up the bow. After repairs, we tied up to a pier. A barge had to tie up to our bow and slowly disassemble the torpedoes in the tubes from the outside. The pieces were forced out of the twenty-four foot long tubes. Long solid steel plugs had to be forced into the tubes over and over, until they were straightened. The inquiry determined that we dove into an uncharted fresh water stream. A submarine is much more buoyant in salt water, but it sinks like a rock in fresh water. Like a plane that hits an air pocket, the submarine reacts the same in fresh water.

I mentioned the lack of knowledge of our coast and shore to show how little we knew about it. How could a vast underwater stream go undetected for so long, and where was its source?

One submarine from our squadron was operating in Long Island Sound, and rammed into something while they were submerged. They surfaced to control their flooding and called to report the damage.

The submarine base sent out our diving barge to help control the flooding, to discover what uncharted object was hit. The divers arrived and began to search below and soon found the object. It was a coal barge. When they scraped off the side, they found out its name. The divers reported the findings to our base, and returned with the damaged submarine.

We later heard that this coal barge had sunk a long time ago.

What startled us was it had sunk in the Great Lakes hundreds of miles away. How could a coal barge sink in Lake Erie, and travel that distance down any river undetected to end up in Long Island Sound? Are there ancient volcanic paths under the continent? This could explain large uncharted fresh water streams flowing into the ocean. I sure am not qualified to answer that question.

How much have we not yet discovered, sitting on the ocean bottom right off our coast?

CHAPTER 18

Wrong Side of the Door

In the spring of 1961, the Submarine Angler submerged on a mission in Long Island Sound, New York. I was on watch in the control room at the twelve-foot long electrical panel. The panel controlled the many weapons and devices throughout the ship. Above it was a manual trip switch for the forward 126 one-ton batteries. In the middle of the room was our Armor Main Compass and DRAI device. These units told us which direction, and where we were at any given time, while submerged or surfaced. On secret missions, I taped over the viewing window of the DRAI Unit, so not even the captain knew our exact location!

Whenever our battle-wise captain came through the control room, I learned to keep one eye on him. He loved to loosen a fuse on the panel, and see how long it took before I figured it out. Below the control room were two rooms: the sonar room, and the pump room. Above me was a hatch to get up into the conning tower, our attack center. Eleven of us stood critical watches here in the control and sonar rooms, while on patrol in the depths. When at battle stations, there were many more people manning the many weapons below and around me.

One day submerged on watch, I heard a very loud boom and

the roar of water rushing in. It sounded like the roaring of a lift in the garage, when a car was lowered. We all looked around for the source of the trouble before it was too late. I stared down into the pump room below me. There was water swirling around and bubbling up fast. I yelled "flooding in the pump room," the only room without a hatch to seal. I slammed shut the after-battery hatch beside me, sealing the rear of the ship off from our control room. The auxiliary man, Don Delisle, slammed the forward-battery hatch, sealing us off from the front-half of the submarine. Above and below, the hatches were quickly shut. Don and I opened the high pressure salvage air valves letting in three thousand pound high pressure air into our space. This air pressure volume drops radically when released from the tanks. The air pressure built up quickly in our sealed off compartment! We screamed as loud as we could to try and equalize the high air pressure against our ears. We were taught this was the quickest way to try and equalize air pressure on our inner ear drums.

I was unable to hear any other scream over the roaring sound of the incoming air and water. My ears pulsated as the pressure got higher and higher. I wondered if the air pressure would build up high enough, before I was covered in ice-cold seawater. Unlike what Hollywood depicts, we had no time to get repair items. Twelve feet of water took less than a few minutes to accumulate.

The blood flowed from my ears as my inner ears burst, pain and fear spread throughout my body. The flooding stopped at a twelve foot depth, filling the pump room up to my ankles. I saw someone looking in at us through the tiny round thick hatch window. We had saved the boat and our lives. Finally, the air pressure inside exceeded the sea pressure and water was forced down and out the ruptured hole. We discovered all that flooding was caused by a blown open two-inch-wide pipe.

We were not very deep. I tried to imagine our fate if we had been deeper. The hole was patched and the air pressure was slowly released into the adjoining compartments. When the pressure was equal on both sides of the hatch, they were reopened. The pain and bleeding from my ears slowed to a dull ache.

Time repaired the holes in my ears but not my hearing. I lost much of my hearing, but consider that much better than sinking and imploding in the depths below.

I looked down into the pump room at the dozens of electric motors and pumps submerged in the cold salt water! All these had to be removed, and I was one of the electricians that had to rebuild them. I survived this event, because GOD had other plans for me that day. I have relived this event too many times in my dreams, and once in a daytime visit to the doctor's office. Our training had taught us to react quickly to save our lives from a watery grave.

CHAPTER 19

David Against Goliath in the Mediterranean Sea

Here Comes the Judge

During War Games, every war movie portrays one group trying to overpower another group. I'll tell you what really happens in a submarine attack! The following account is what happened to me, while on board The USS Entemedor SS340—a 1940 World War II diesel-powered submarine.

In the summer of 1962, Vice Admiral Rickover, the father of the nuclear submarine navy, ordered a no-holds-barred war game. Our submarine was ordered to cross the Atlantic Ocean, and attack the Six Fleet Battle Group guarding the entrance to the Mediterranean Sea.

Halfway across the ocean, we crossed the international dateline. This is a line that, when crossed west to east, you lose one day. Friday becomes Thursday and Saturday becomes Friday. Here, we stopped and the old salts disappeared and reappeared in costume. All of us who never crossed the international dateline didn't have a clue what was about to happen. We were captured, and forced to pay 'Our Tribute to King Neptune!'

Neptune was the heaviest man on board who crossed before. He sat in the mess hall on his throne, on top of a table dressed up in his regalia. He had a clean white mop for hair, and was girded with a towel around his bulging, multi-tiered belly. Smeared all over his huge belly was mustard, tabasco, and disgusting hot sauces. His court was comprised of our old salty chief petty officers. The brims of their hats were turned backwards, and written in marker on each forehead was the word **guilty**. Obviously, they were an impartial jury?

One by one, we were captured from around the boat, and brought in to be judged by Neptune's Court. I was brought in through a double line of sailors chanting guilty, guilty over and over. The lead chief rose up and read aloud a bunch of charges, and then turned to the panel of judges—our chiefs. He shouted out loud for all to hear, "How find you"? The chiefs circled around and looked at me, turned and called out in unison, "guilty, guilty." The crew's cheers were deafening. "What be his punishment?" the jury called out. The whole crew chanted, "Kiss Neptune's Belly, Neptune's Belly!" I was dragged over, and pushed down on my knees in front of Neptune. Everyone chanted as Neptune grabbed my head, and smeared my face through the red and yellow slimy mess. Then all my shipmates cheered, because I was one of them again. Now, it was my turn to join in, and catch someone else.

When all sailors were finally caught and mortified, it was time to "Splice the Main Brace." This happens when everyone lines up in front of two huge pots with a coffee cup. The cook pours five gallons of one hundred and eighty proof pure alcohol, between each huge five-gallon pot and tops it off with orange juice. The smiling cook stirs the brew slowly, as we all look on in anticipation. We chant as he ladles a liberal amount of this mixture into each cup that passes by. When I consumed my witches brew, I ran back to the end of the line for another cup. Two trips and Neptune's Nectar was all gone, but with all the laughing and stories who cared! Our bonding was even closer than before—now back to work. Seven more days of rocking and rolling in the North Atlantic, and we arrived at the entrance of the Mediterranean Sea.

The Sixth Fleet guarded the entrance, and monitored any ship entering or leaving. The Navy thought a World War II sub wouldn't have a chance when attacking a Nuclear-powered Aircraft Carrier and its fleet, guess again!

Our Mission was to sneak up to the Nuclear Enterprise Group and attack. Through the periscope, we could see destroyers, cruisers, planes, and helicopters buzzing around like a wasp nest, ready to pounce on us. There was over a hundred enemy ships, and planes protecting the USS Enterprise CVN65. The sky was full of helicopters, reconnaissance planes, and fighters. We would test just how vulnerable the U.S. Navy Sixth Fleet was. We had one week to find a weak spot, if any, and penetrate through their lines of defense.

Our 1940 submarine attacked the most modern nuclear navy in the world, but we had a secret weapon—an experienced, WW II battle-ready captain.

Before dawn, we submerged and went to battle stations. It didn't take long before we found our main target. Through the periscope, we spotted the carrier, a sitting duck with all her ducklings circling around in a protecting pattern. The thirteen destroyers and two much larger cruisers circled around her, including dozens of aircraft that filled the sky, searching for us. If we were detected, they would depth charge us, and game over. They used smaller depth charges that make a lot of noise, and shake your fillings but wouldn't sink us.

We travelled around outside of the task force, putting the periscope up and down looking for a weak spot. Their radar makes a complete revolution in fourteen seconds, so we had to make quick observations. The captain scanned the group, and relayed the information to the attack center below. The Officers Ward Room, the attack center, was my battle station. I stood behind a large Plexiglas wall. In the middle of this transparent wall was a three-foot-diameter see-through wheel. It had many diagonal lines on it. I spun the wheel, and marked on the window the compass bearings called down to me by phone. Measuring the distance between the targets, Xs showed the direction of travel, and how fast they were going. I marked Xs, where the targets were on this grid, and printed numbers backwards so the officers could read them correctly from the opposite side. The officers studied all the marks, and formed a plan of attack. Their information was sent by me back to the captain, and fed into the conning tower computers. The computers indicated to the captain a final attack solution.

Each time we attacked, a destroyer's sonar detected us and swung from their circling pattern to depth charge us. We dove deep quickly and went to ultra quiet. We soon disappeared in the depths below, and stopped the propellers, floating on an ocean thermal layer undetectable. I heard the ping, ping, ping from the ship going over us, then the whooshing sound from their propellers. The helicopters were lowering a dumpster-size sonar dome on a cable, trying to locate us. P B Y RECONNAISSANCE planes flew a search pattern, and dropped three-foot flashlight-looking devices with an antenna on top. These extended the sonar searching range, and returned signals up to them. The whole picture resembled a nest of angry bees, shooting in all directions looking for an intruder. The captain watched each path the ships took, when they swung away from the group pattern. We closed in as deadly as a snake, weaving back and forth, closing in pursuit of its prey. We got close enough to simulate firing a torpedo, and we sank a cruiser. After firing, we called out a code bearing on the underwater telephone, and they acknowledged being sunk. The cruiser, a premier weapon, was now out of the game. So, we turned and sank a tanker. The tanker refuels the fleet at sea; this was a costly mistake on their part. You don't want to run out of gas at sea! We continued our attack, and two more were destroyed and put out of action.

At sunset, the captain had another trick up his sleeve to confuse the enemy. He called for an electric razor to be sent up into the conning tower. I thought it was crazy to shave at this time, but he had a different plan for it. Just as before, a destroyer detected us and headed straight at us, but this time we didn't dive deep. The captain turned on our underwater speaker and the electric razor. He held the running razor high, and ran across the conning tower to the speaker. The razor made the same sound as a torpedo. The destroyer heard the sound, and thought we had fired a torpedo right at them and radically turned away. In all the confusion of turning ships trying to avoid each other, we surfaced and turned on our running lights. Our tiny submarine turned straight at the Nuclear Carrier, it's as long as the height of the Empire State building. Our submarine silhouette with lights on, is the same as a destroyer in low light. We joined the circling ships, and steamed right up to the aircraft carrier. In quick succession at point blank range, we fired four simulated torpedoes straight into the side of the carrier. We were just five football-field-lengths away, and caught them with their pants down. A 1942 diesel submarine had outwitted a nuclear task force.

We sunk 550,000 tons of war ships in just twenty-four hours. The Entemedor officers and crew were given the Marjorie Starret award, a peace-time cash prize for excellence. We set a new peace-time world record for tonnage sunk. We painted a large white E on the side of our submarine's sail, the superstructure above the deck. The Entemedor was the "Number One Submarine in the Atlantic Fleet."

CHAPTER 20

My Three-City Tour of Spain

After travelling three thousand miles across the Atlantic, we stopped at Rota, Spain to top off our fuel tanks. Our submarine had an eleven thousand mile range.

While in the Mediterranean Sea, our submarine had to back up to the pier called med mooring. We always face the open sea ready to escape if needed. I rigged the electrical Mediterranean light strands. The sixty-watt bulbs are a foot apart and are strung from the sub's bow up to our highest point, and all the way to the farthest point back. All American warships have to rig their lights the same way, while in Mediterranean ports. At night, these glowing lights show the United States presence in a very obvious and intimidating way.

Only fifty percent of the crew can leave the boat at any one time. The submarine has to be ready for any emergency—if it happens, we leave and submerge awaiting orders. I looked forward to only working an eight-hour day in port, instead of the sixteen plus hours at sea.

Finally at liberty, I left the ship with my friend "Animal," a second class electrician, and soon found out why they called him this nickname. He spoke the language and promised to show me the ropes, since he had been to Spain many times. Our first stop was the local enlisted men's club for shots of vodka. I seldom drank and then only a beer, because I wasn't twenty-one yet. This new freedom I welcomed, but learned to regret.

We left the club after many shots of vodka, and hailed a taxi. Animal told the cab driver where we wanted to go, and to get us something to drink. The cab drove off and bounced down a dirt road, and then turned off into a field. It became a Disney Land ride. We hung on while travelling across rows of grape vine mounds. I thought for sure we were going to get mugged in this out of the way place. The ride stopped at a tiny old barnboard, weathered shack in the middle of a field. Animal and the taxi driver went into the windowless, unpainted, gray colored shack. I waited, fearful that someone with a machete was going to come out, and run at me. Time went by and finally Animal and the taxi driver came out singing in Spanish with five bottles of wine. We each took two bottles and gave one bottle to the driver. They were finished long before we reached the local town of Cadiz, Spain.

The cobblestone ancient streets were too narrow for us to pass all the way into town, so the taxi stopped and we headed off. I walked by many houses without any solid doors or windows, only strands of beads hanging in the openings. I couldn't see a wooden building anywhere—only one-story adobe style structures, attached to each other by a common wall with stick-covered roofs. We walked along and stopped at each bar we passed. Animal and I had a double shot of cognac with a beer chaser; he said it was tradition. Tired, we stopped at a bar to get out of the sun and hundred-degree heat. Soon, we each had a pretty young senorita on our laps and we joined in the singing, while buying drinks for everyone. I was having the time of my life, dancing and laughing. All was going great. Animal was singing the loudest and laughing with everyone in the bar. Suddenly, Animal just sucker-punched the girl on his lap and laughed. I just looked in shock, but the men in the bar jumped up in horror. Animal and I quickly ran out of the bar with many people in quick pursuit. Now, I knew how he got that nickname. Alcohol turned him from Dr. Jekyll into Mr. Hyde without any warning.

Fortunately, we didn't run into any of President Franco's Guard. We had been warned, if we got into trouble. The guards grabbed you and threw you into a straw-covered floor cell, or they shot you depending on their mood. No trial is expected, and you are never heard of again.

Each small town had a group of guards that lived in tents right in its center, and their word was law. The guards strutted about with a black Dixie cup hat with a wide fan in the back. Hanging from their shoulder was an automatic rifle; you knew not to mess with them. Franco kept each town in check, and the obviously very poor people lived in fear.

We headed to the American bar to join all the rest of our crew. Upon arrival, we yelled to our friends and ordered a drink. The word BAR was a major exaggeration. Just three lower fieldstone walls attached against a larger building with a see-through stick roof. In one corner was a waist-high wall with a through hole by my feet for expelling fluids out into the street. The bar area had a series of large wooden barrels tipped on end with some boards across them. On top of the unpainted boards were multiple bottles, no glasses, mixes or ice. You bought a bottle; the bartender wiped off the top with his dirty apron, and handed it to you. The jug was at room temperature in the one hundred plus degree air.

The crew carried on "as The Pirates of Old" laughing and singing, tossing our bottles through the air to someone else around the circle. Occasionally, it missed and smashed on the cobblestone floor. We laughed all the louder. We only lacked a patch over one eye, and a parrot on our shoulder. Yo ho ho and a bottle of rum, bring me a wench!

Animal wanted to go to the town of Herez, where souvenirs are cheap. We hired a taxi and headed out to shop for bargains; singing all the way. The taxi couldn't get down the narrow dirt street, so we got out and headed to the town square. We walked across the dusty square right by a dried up fountain, and entered the only store. I entered through the beaded doorway into an adobe-style dwelling with just one beaded window. Stealing was not a problem here; their Dictator Franco had swift and final judgment laws. Any infraction, and they threw you in prison to rot—or stood you against the wall to be shot.

Inside the store were wooden pegs driven into the mud walls with boards on top. Piles of trinkets were loosely scattered on top of the unpainted boards with the price on a torn piece of paper. We picked out some knives upon which were bull-fighting scenes, and some sword-letter openers. The ratcheted knife blades had different bull fighting scenes engraved on them in bright colors. The owner wrapped all the items in an old newspaper, and handed the bundle to us—there are no bags here.

We stepped outside, and were greeted by twenty-five to thirty Spanish peasants. The angry beady-eyed crowd began to circle around us. We took out our recently bought knives, and quickly opened the blades. Back-to-back with knives drawn, we forced our way through the crowd and a space opened. The look on their faces left no doubt we were not welcome here. It was a good thing we were both over two hundred pounds, Animal is six foot two and I'm six feet tall. Our size and knives made us look very intimidating, thank GOD! Once through the crowd, we ran to the taxi. It sped off down the narrow street with us laughing nervously all the way to the American bar. If either of us had panicked, our bodies would be lying in some sun-baked field. I can always count on a submariner for support.

I learned this hostility toward Americans was universal through-out most of the Mediterranean countries I visited. The only exception was major cities and the country of Greece. In Greece to hurt a tourist is a capital offence. In the four months in the Mediterranean, our crew were jumped, robbed, drugged, beaten, and shot, just because we wore our uniform. The captain explained to us, that if we were caught out of uniform we would be treated as spies. Even I was drugged, and woke up in a village square with the taste of kerosene in my mouth, and an empty wallet.

Meanwhile, after returning to the American bar, we laughingly told our buddies about our close encounter. It's just another experience, I put in my memories and survival skill book. The rest of the night, I don't remember because the drinks caught up to me.

The next day my shipmates told me I had a lot of fun, but I don't have a clue. They told stories of me bull fighting on my hands and knees in my dress white uniform, these events were vali-dated by scrapes on my hands and knees. I have never been that drunk or sick in my life. I promised myself to never, ever drink like that again, so help me God!

The next day was *hangover hell*, if I tried to move my body it would not respond. Partying looked like so much fun in the movies, but I learned a painful life lesson that I never forgot. I suffered through the day in my bunk, unable to sit or stand. My boss, Chief reprimanded me for not being able to perform my job. He could have shot me, and I would have thanked him. I just laid there unable to clean myself, and smelling very foul. I was given an extra weekend duty, when all my buddies would go ashore at the next port. With only few days off per month, to lose any of them hurt me the most. It was torture working below decks in a metal can with one hundred degree heat penetrating my every pore. It was painful thinking of the scantily clad women roaming along the beach in front of the submarine.

At dawn the following day, I took down and put away the long strands of Mediterranean lights. The engines roared awake, as the crew prepared to go to sea. We released the mooring lines, and the three thousand pound propellers turned in the clear blue water leaving behind many memories. Over the horizon the sub submerged, off on another secret mission, never knowing where, or if we would return; this was the life I chose.

CHAPTER **21**

The Rock of Gibraltar

The entrance to the Mediterranean Sea is guarded by the English port of Gibraltar. The famous Rock of Gibraltar is a huge butter-yellow, pocked-marked, volcanic rock jutting up out of the Mediterranean Ocean. This barren rock is studded with adobe style buildings that have open windows and doorways. Standing on the back deck of our ship as we passed into the harbor, I could see English sailors in their short pants and shirts. I envied them, as we stood in long pants and sleeved uniforms in the hundred degree heat. At the water's edge were people stretched out on beach towels on the hard stone, in between pock-marked depressed crevices enjoying the sun. We tied up to an old, wooden pier, and liberty was announced.

Luckily, I had time off to explore the area. I walked up the hacked-out solid rock road into the city. The lack of trees and grass was a stark reality of this barren landscape. I entered the edge of the city, and heard tiny bells ringing. A car stopped near me, and the driver got out and kneeled in the street. I saw a small group of altar boys dressed in black and white robes walking down the sidewalk followed by a priest. The lead altar boy was ringing a cluster of silver bells, and the others carried lit candles. The priest was holding a covered cup, bringing the last rites to a dying person. People knelt on the sidewalk and in the street, and blessed themselves as the procession passed by them. I have never seen that much faith in public before, or since from any people around the globe. I knelt with the rest, and felt at peace.

I continued up the steep road, and passed a small shoe shop with a boot sign hanging in front. I looked through the open stone-framed window at the lone cobbler making shoes. He looked up from his shoe form, and invited me in. The cobbler said that he could make a custom pair of sandals for me in a short time. I looked at a few samples, and was surprised that each pair had arch supports and raised, soft, curved leather, caressing the toe area in front. We talked for a while, as he measured my feet for a custom pair of sandals. I left and continued along the winding street to the top of the hill.

There stood a pale, time-weathered limestone church decorated with intricate carvings on the facade and doorway. Inside the unlocked empty church, I saw no seating anywhere. A lit candle stood by the altar. The only other light came from an alcove off to one side with a gold crowned bejeweled statue of Mary. I could feel something like a mother's warmth closing in around my shoulders, and I felt at home in this ancient church.

I continued along the wavy road and spotted a store with large, glass windows. There were two boxes of America chocolate bars staring back at me, a miracle find in this far away place. At sea in a couple of weeks, anyone would kill for a chocolate bar. I bought both boxes and hid them at the bottom of my drawstring shoulder bag, dreaming how great they would taste in the future aboard ship.

I returned after a while to the cobbler, and put on my custom sandals. My feet were caressed in glove-soft leather, my new sandals felt more like a comfortable pair of old slippers.

A week later at sea, I was ordered to show a movie in the forward torpedo room. As the ship projectionist, this was one of my more enjoyable functions. I slipped into the after battery sleeping area to recover two candy bars from my locker. They were quickly hidden in my shirt pocket to be enjoyed later in the darkness of the movie. I brought the movie reels, and projector to the forward torpedo room. Sailors were in any space available, lying on the steel floor or across the top of torpedoes. The lucky ones rested on bunks. Each movie had two or three 16-millimeter reels. I started one reel, and silently enjoyed my candy bar in the dark.

When the first reel ended, I turned on the lights and changed to another reel and started the projector. In the dark, I bit into my second candy bar and felt something moving on the back of my hand. I stepped into the next lighted room to examine my hand, and saw ants crawling all over the back of my hand and up one sleeve. I looked into the candy wrapper and saw that it was full of ants. My stomach clinched as I ran back to my locker, and pulled out the boxes of chocolate. All of the chocolate bars in each box were covered with ants running all over. I wondered how many ants I had eaten, while enjoying the movie.

Back at the movie, I told the guys and they all laughed like hell, watching me as I wiggled and rubbed my stomach. To them, it was better than the movie! They said it served me right for not sharing the candy bars with everyone. It became a horror movie for me, as my stomach felt movement for several more days.

I became the butt of many jokes. "Can you feel the little ones kicking?" Or, "Your shirt is moving." And then there was, "Don't bug me." All common jabs were given to me for some time. I regretted my actions.

We were one big friendly-teasing family, enjoying our common life in our sixteen-foot, wide-steel tube home.

CHAPTER 22

All Ashore That's Going Ashore, A Time to Play

It was the summer of 1962 and we were heading into Toulon, France. Unfortunately, the entire rest of the 10,000 man Sixth Fleet was joining us. We had eight hours to spend one month's pay, and then back to the regiment of military life.

Upon arriving, we did not have to moor out in the harbor with the rest of the fleet. We just blew water out from our tanks, which made us rise up and we backed up to a local pier. This was called med mooring. The boat always had to be pointed out toward the open ocean, just in case.

Our landing was a comedy of errors that still makes me laugh after all these years. I was the rear deck-phone talker. My job was to relay orders from the bridge officer to my line handlers. I also estimated the distance to the pier, and relayed it to the bridge as the sub backed up. The dress white uniforms shone in the midday sun as a dozen men stood at attention on deck. The boat backed up slowly, using one propeller at a time, wiggling back into position like a woman into tight jeans. Each mooring line's slack was pulled in, then the sub pivoted off that line, and we pulled on the other line, closing the gap to the pier.

A junior officer was in charge and very nervous, leaning way over the bridge looking at us. The captain watched his every move, along with some local French families who came to enjoy this special event. It was taking a lot of time, because we don't normally moor this way and he had never done it before. The orders came over my headphones, "put over the brow." (The brow was our 16-foot long, walking plank). I repeated the order, and added "but we are thirty-five feet from the pier!"

"Put over the brow!" he reordered. I reluctantly gave the order, and the blank look from my fellow sailors reaffirmed my thoughts. The sixteen-foot plank made a great splash, sinking down twenty-five feet onto the sandy bottom.

The roar of laughter from the spectators was deafening, as a chief petty officer came running back in his dress white uniform. I told him about the orders, as he looked down into the clear watery depths. The engines were still running, and we had to keep using the propellers to stay in place. One of my line-handling sailors was ordered to dive down, and attach a small line onto the brow. He took off his dress white jumper and shoes, then dove in and swam over, took a deep breath and submerged to his target. He attempted to tie on the rope, not an easy task on a breath of air. The sailor dove down over and over beside the six-foot high propellers. A very dangerous job, so close to sometimes-moving propellers. Each time the diver surfaced, the viewing crowd would cheer. All they needed was some popcorn for the show. A half hour passed by with no luck, while now three sailors took turns diving down. An officer came back to survey the problem, and said "Chief, get it done."

The chief petty officer took off his dress white jacket, full of medals and laid it down on the black deck on top of his shiny shoes. The balding, old warrior jumped, and made one big cannon ball splash. He surfaced with a small swatch of black hair hanging off to one side exposing a large bald area. He grabbed the rope, took a couple of deep breaths and dove deep. When he surfaced, the crowd cheers were deafening. A few more breaths and down he descended again and again till the line was attached. The chief's thumbs-up brought the crowd to an Olympic roar. The brow was pulled up, and the submarine backed up to just five feet from the pier. The still wet brow was laid from the stern to the pier, and our ship insignia tarp was tied onto the pipes along its side.

I had duty that day. Because I was six feet tall and two hundred pounds, I was assigned to shore patrol, the military police in town. I reported to a local building to join eleven other beefy sailors on the riot police squad. We were given a black shore patrol arm band with S P on it, and a webbed-white belt with a billy club attached to keep the peace. The whole fleet of 10,000 men had about one million dollars total to spend in eight hours ashore. This amount of money guaranteed lots of liquor and wild women action—it was not going to be a quiet night!

In Toulon, France, there were three places for 'social interaction': First, the long sandy beaches, which were filled with bikini-clad woman. Second, the "Black Cat Bar," here alcohol wasn't "the only thing for sale." And third, the many small shops, which lined along the beach front, where you could buy all the latest Parisian clothes and items.

Whenever I went on liberty, I got as far away from the salt water as I could. I had $100 to spend in a place where a loaf of bread costs one franc, only one third of a penny. There were 365 francs to one American dollar in 1962.

While on my trip throughout the Mediterranean, this "country bumpkin" got an eye-full of their different lifestyles. Seeing women in a Playboy magazine was one thing, but encountering hundreds of nearly naked woman after weeks at sea was entirely different. They changed right on the beach under their loose robes, exposing their well-tanned trim bodies.

The expression "two dollar, two dollar" was the cost of a private, self-guided tour by a local prostitute. Prostitution was legal and too normal of a way of life for some girls and their families. These girls were inspected by their government doctors every two weeks. They had a little book stamped with their "government inspection mark."

Each French sailor was paid $2.50 a month plus two tickets to a whore house of his choice. Greek sailors were paid $3.50 plus two tickets to his choice of a whore house. Depending on which country, a prostitute either worked in a group setting, or took you up to her room. After meeting his "date," one of my buddies was taken to her house and introduced to her family first, and then taken up to her room! There, hanging from her bed post, were Rosary beads and a Cross hung over the bed. His conscience overturned his desire, and he quickly retreated to consume more alcohol.

In Sardinia, Italy, some girls stood in doorways wearing long coats in the over 100-degree heat. They flashed their naked bodies as men walked by. Their coats were opened and sexual acts were completed right there. Some of the crew went out to a local pizza house, where food was not on the menu. A long corridor was next to the bar with light fixtures sticking out from the walls every few feet. The Madame took you down the corridor and pulled a light fixture, and the wall opened up showing each different type of girl. Just window shopping, except it was not for clothes.

Another adjustment for me was the coed bathrooms. Even in five star restaurants when I relieved myself, I sometimes ended up standing next to a woman or child. The first time it happened to me, I nearly ruined my equipment thinking I was in the wrong room. The Europe idea of the human body is less perverted than here in the states. "A naked body was just another outfit."

One night in Toulon, I was assigned to patrol "Pig Alley," a pervert's dream, with eleven other shore patrolmen. Pig Alley was the local term for a four-block-long area of prostitutes. Two to three story buildings stood side-by-side with windows full of half naked women. In each window was a beautiful woman of every size and color, shaking their 'bee bees' or—oh my goodness—breasts and bottoms. Six shore patrolmen stood shoulder to shoulder across one opening of this four block area. The other six of the riot patrol stood across, way down at the opposite end. Our mission was to keep the 5,000 drunken, horny sailors and marines with pockets full of money from reaching all these naked women. This area had a high incidence of socially transmitted diseases, and the Navy did not want them to cripple the fleet.

I was standing for about an hour in the 100 degree heat just watching the show. I would have loved to have gone into one of those houses, and had a cold beer—yes, a cold beer!

All the streets in Toulon were cobblestone, and "Pig Alley" was halfway up a hill going off to one side. A woman came running down the hill out of breath yelling, "Several men are beating up a sailor and he's all bloody!" We all took out our billy clubs, and ran up the hill in hot pursuit. We were a couple of blocks up, when we heard the sound of hundreds of shoes pounding the cobblestone street. I turned and saw a blur of white uniformed drunken sailors running into Pig Alley. They flowed into the waiting arms of an equal amount of waiting naked woman. Out of breath, we stood in helpless dismay and slowly walked back down to our positions, determined not to be duped again. The sailors had to come back out, but how could the six of us stop the stampede of hundreds of drunken sailors? This was **"SPARTACUS"** all over again, six warriors across a small opening trying to stop an invading hoard.

A short time later we heard a loud clattering sound of beating wheels against the cobblestone street. I wondered if it was another trick, as the sound became louder and louder right to us. A two-wheeled cart suddenly appeared from around the bend, turned backwards with handles dragging on the ground rolling down the middle of the street. In front stood a sailor posed like Napoleon with one hand over his heart, and the other shading his eyes. The cart flew by us in a second, and a few hundred yards below turned abruptly, crashing through a store-front window. Two of us ran down to help him, but he was laughing his head off without a scratch. "God protects drunks and fools." The other patrolman led him off in handcuffs with the drunken fool laughing the whole time.

We five shore patrolmen were still laughing about the event, when I saw the other patrolmen at the opposite end of the alley running up the hill. A whistle blew and a mass exodus of hundreds of sailors and marines charged out of the whore houses. They ran out the opposite exit, and disappeared in all directions. This became a non-Spartacus event.

The next day, I had to work aboard the submarine doing electrical repairs until five o'clock. I left with some friends to take in the sights. We found a five-story high night club with lots of cold beer. It had a double mahogany S-shaped bar on the bottom floor. Along the sides were tables with pretty women everywhere! A huge dance floor was in the center, and I could see through the huge ceiling opening many floors above me with doors to rooms. You could buy drinks at the bar and dance with a girl from a table, or travel up into one of the rooms with a woman and bottle. I sang and drank till late that night, and then returned to the sub totally stress free.

The following day, I worked my shift and looked forward to a return trip to the club. My buddy and I got off early, and went into town to check out the night club. We walked up, and stared at the night club's machine gunned walls. We peeked through the boarded-up front door and windows, and saw the whole place was shot up. Bullet holes were through the bar, furniture, and walls, broken glass all over the floor. We walked around back, and saw a couple of the girls that worked there. They told us the Algerian Rebels found out the U.S. Navy had been there, and shot the club to pieces as a warning. This changed my perspective regarding the invincibility of the United States. We left and kept our eyes open as we headed to another bar. I thought the U.S. was king of the hill, and I could go anywhere unharmed, but everyone does not share that same opinion!

The next day our submarine left port on another secret mission. My mind was full of good memories, and the bikini-clad girls left behind.

CHAPTER 23

Cannes, France

Our submarine drove to anchor right off the beaches of Cannes, France. The crescent line of high rise hotels spread out before us, with palm trees scattered on the butter-yellow beaches. Best of all, it was the Cannes Film Festival time. This event drew all the movie stars, and hundreds of beautiful bikini-clad women to our area.

Our submarine started into the maze of Navy ships, and right by the nuclear aircraft carrier USS Forestall. We travelled right under the overhanging side edge of this mammoth ship. When we finally passed her, I could see full-sized cars driving around on her huge deck. The scale of our boat to her was like standing in the middle of a football stadium, looking in awe at the height and breadth of it all. The carrier was almost as long as the height of the Empire State building with a crew of six thousand sailors. Later, inside her, I travelled the maze of numbered-arrow paths all color coded, so you wouldn't get lost. This nuclear carrier has enough power to run all of Manhattan, New York in an emergency!

We anchored just five hundred yards off the bikini-clad main beach, thank you, GOD! While standing on deck, I watched a hydrofoil ferry leave from a nearby pier at high speed. When it sounded a horn," doo dah, doo dahhh," the huge ship popped up, and out of the water. It took off, and was soon speeding about sixty miles an hour with a huge cocks cone of water spraying up behind. Hundreds of people were peering out of its wrap around windows like a Disney ride. It was simply awesome to watch a huge ship travel so very fast!

We were close enough to the beach to see women waving at us, and some came out in little paddle boats to take our picture. These well tanned, bikini clad girls acted coy and yelled to us in French, which I didn't understand. Their sign gestures had me posing for pictures as they giggled, and we enjoyed each other's company. Three years of high school French, and I still had to use gestures to communicate with these beautiful girls.

I rigged our Mediterranean Lights, "like a string of Chinese lanterns," and scanned the horizon sitting fifty-feet up on top of the submarine. I turned to look in all directions. In one direction, I saw the whole Sixth Fleet, and the other palm tree covered beaches in front of tall curve-shaped buildings. Each hotel had their own color-coded umbrellas that staked out the beach in front of them. White jacketed waiters, like a flock of penguins, brought tall cold drinks to the people under those colorful shaded spots.

I heard the thundering sounds of racing boats coming straight at me. The submarine became a turning marker for dozens of high speed boats. It was a thrill to see these long sea racing boats skipping across the ocean. Each racer had several drivers to control the high powered boats, as they turned in a wide arc, skipping sideways, throwing up a huge wall of water around us.

Our Sixth Fleet was moored way out in the bay, and everyone

had to wait for the small liberty boats to pull alongside and bring them ashore. It was difficult to jump aboard the rocking liberty boat sober, but returning after several drinks was a comical but dangerous task. One sailor on another ship got his leg caught between the liberty boat and ship, shattering it like an egg. We were the last to be picked up, because we were not part of the task force. Our missions were separate, because we could hardly sneak around with the Sixth Fleet floating on top of us.

I headed for the beach to see the beautiful bikini-clad women. I took out my new eight-millimeter camera and wound it up, and looked through the view finder. I slowly panned the camera across the beach filming beautiful women everywhere. These goddesses just removed clothing from under their loose moo, moo dresses and put on their suits. The filming with my six by eight inch metal-cased camera drew a lot of attention from the photographers, using old fashioned wooden box 16 mm cameras. Their large cameras on top of a tripod had to be dragged through the sand. Many of them offered big money to buy my new technology hand-held camera. I bought it at the aircraft carrier store, but I couldn't buy another one before they left port. My camera only drawback was that after filming twenty-five feet, a total of two and one-half minutes run time, I had to get to a dark area and open the side to turn over the sixteen millimeter film. I then could expose another twenty-five feet, find a dark place, and put in a new film. I bought prepaid mailers and when processed, they went to my mother's house. I received all of them!

After all the eye candy, I went to visit the many small shops that peppered the beach front. I stopped at a bakery to buy fresh bread and goodies. A French bread stick was almost two feet long, and two inches thick but only cost one franc, "one third of a penny." Everything was baked right in front of you in a huge wood-fired brick oven, and the taste was awesome. Later that day, I bought a pizza cooked the same way; no pan, cooked right on the bricks in the oven center with glowing red coals on each side. It was the very best I ever have had. My mouth still waters just thinking of it today.

I went into a woman's dress shop to buy my future wife a Paris creation. The clerk helped me and showed a gorgeous, off white three-piece suit with a light blue flower pattern across the top. I fell in love with it, and she asked what size I wanted. The clerk used metric sizes that I couldn't relate to. I showed with my hands about what was her waist size. When she said bust size," I cupped my hands but stopped before I embarrassed myself." I felt the heat spreading up my face and turned quickly, pointing at a woman about her size. I bought the items and knew she would be excited with a three-piece Paris suit.

Just two blocks behind the palm tree hotels were adobe style shacks with an open window casing and door. A butcher had pegs on his outside wall with plucked chickens hanging heads-down in one hundred degree heat. I wondered how the French people didn't get sick eating them. I stepped inside his shop to get cold cuts, and on the counter saw what I thought was pepper-coated meat. To my horror when the butcher moved his hand, the pepper flew up in the air.

I passed an old WW II large cement bunker on the side of a hill that had tables down inside. I stepped out of the sun into the cool dim light and sat down. When my eyes adjusted, I saw an-other sailor and ordered him a beer. We talked awhile and I told him I was from Boston, and he replied the same. Sailors from the Northeast always say "Boston," because of the many small towns and cities. I was from a town of two thousand and his town was not that much larger. Actually, he was from Methuen, Mass and I'm from Salem, New Hampshire just ten miles apart. Thirty-five hundred miles from home, and I met someone who lived only ten miles from my house. We enjoyed a couple of beers together, and I moved on to enjoy more sights. The golden sun was setting on the yellow beach, as I moved down to the shore before dark.

I headed off to find my shipmates and have a cold beer. I finally found many of my buddies at a small bar, far removed from the sea. Many of the French bars were claimed by a ship's crew, when enough of their sailors end up there. Each ship or boat attached their drinking flag up on the wall, and started singing their submarine or Navy song. We all drank freely but loved to raid a rival's bar, and steal their drinking flag to display in our bar. We would be singing when a white blur of sailors would rush in a side door, and try to get our flag. Resulting in a pushing match that would be replayed later that night at their bar. Our flag was a crimson red silk beauty with a Black Panther in the middle, and a raised arm throwing a torpedo and a beer stein in the other hand. Mack's Marauders was printed below it in large bold black letters. "I didn't travel three thousand miles to look into the bottom of a glass!" I left to explore the countryside away from the bars.

After another day of duty, I had more time off to go with my buddies. We decided to travel as a group into town, and find a nice club with a girlie show. We found a great high class night club, and settled in for a fun-filled evening. There were beautiful girls serving drinks to each table at sky high prices. We didn't care, because we had more money than time to spend it. Eight hours off every other day in port, and then out to sea for weeks at a time, let me save plenty of money. That night we had many, many laughs and drinks, then suddenly the lights went off. When they came on, we saw our waitresses in can-can outfits.

They started to dance and scream with the live music playing the typical fast-paced can-can style. It was a jazzed up version with the girls doing a bump and grind action right in front of our table. They enjoyed the whistles and calls as they circled our table and put on our hats. We enjoyed the extra attention, and they knew it meant big tips for them later. The music stopped and everything went black again. When the lights came back on, they announced Bridgett their star performer. She walked about singing in French playing up to all the men in her long sexy white silk outfit and gloves. Her light brown hair was all curled up in Athena type scrolls, held in place by sparkling jeweled combs.

One of our guys left for the men's room after too many beers. He was gone for a while and we were going to check on him, but only after her song. The lights went black again, and then a bright spotlight shone on Bridgett. She pulled out one comb and then the other, shaking her hair as it fell down across her breasts. Slowly turning she looked lovingly at us, starting to dance and disrobe in the spotlight. First one long silk glove was slowly lowered to the music's beat, and thrown into the darkness behind her. Then the other was teasingly lowered, and thrown into the darkness.

It landed right in front of our very drunk friend, just returning, and standing behind her in the dark. He picked up the glove and started dancing around in the dim light mocking her. To our surprise, he slowly started to slide the glove up his arm to the beat of the music right over his uniform. As she removed each item and threw it into the darkness behind her; he picked it up and danced around to the beat of the music, then provocatively slid it on. He slowly pulled her small tossed skirt over his white pants up to his knees. When her bra came off, he shuffled over in beat with music, and put the two tasseled cups over his white jumper top.

The whole crowd started laughing, whistling, clapping, and just going nuts, as he turned coyly with the music. All of this attention boosted her energy, and she really got into it. Bridgett spiraled around in her pasties and g string to our delight. When her routine was over, the lights came on. She stood there with her arms in the air to a standing ovation. Little did she know, it was for the sailor with all her clothes on in reverse over his uniform. He stood behind her, posed with both of his arms up in the air in a playboy pose.

We had a great night and all the girls made a great deal of money! It was the type of night to remember, and was retold over and over.

CHAPTER 24

Sardinia, Italy

The island of Sardinia, Italy is a beautiful tree-studded country with low rolling hills and inviting people. We moored right in the downtown alongside wooden piers, behind a sea wall made of old iron anchors and rocks. Little naked children were laughing and diving into the sea, showing their well browned bodies.

This was the most peaceful spot I had seen in the entire Mediterranean area. The *Entemedor* was the only Navy ship in port, and this meant prices would stay low. A local official came on board, and changed some of our money into their lire currency. Another sub was supposed to meet us, so the radioman called them to report we had moored. He found out they were twenty miles away tied up in the wrong port. Their boat had to stay there, since his crew was already off on liberty.

I walked over the brow onto the pier into the shady downtown area. Everywhere were ancient stone buildings on tree-studded winding streets. It looked just like a European calendar with a century's old unchanged atmosphere. There were no signs on shops or streets anywhere.

Looking through a small doorway, there appeared a long well-shined bar. The lone bartender looked up, as I hopped up on a stool and ordered a beer. Fortunately, the word beer sounds the same in all countries. He spoke no English and I no Italian, so he showed different bottles to make my choice. I gave my smallest Italian bill to him, and his eyes opened wide. The bar tender gestured to me, did I have anything smaller. I spread out my bills, and showed him that it was my smallest bill. He took the bill and left the bar holding his finger up saying "una momento, una momento," leaving me all alone in this quiet bar sipping a cold beer. The bill was the equivalent of two dollars American. He returned after about twenty minutes with a fist full of bills and coins. To my surprise the quart bottle of beer left me with a wallet full of bills, and a pocket full of coins. Still more coins were all over the bar and couldn't fit in my only pocket. So, I gave them to the bartender, who kept thanking me over and over. He followed me out of the bar bending and thanking me. I discovered later the going rate for beer was pennies.

Wandering around the back streets, eight to ten-year-old boys soon surrounded me begging for cigarettes. They were very poorly clothed in torn tee shirts or short pants. No one had both pieces of clothing, and even fewer had sandals. I moved my wallet, staying on my guard as they jumped up all around me. I passed out my cigarettes one at a time till the pack was empty.

One boy came back trying to get another cigarette, and I asked him why he smoked? He told me in his broken English he didn't. The tobacco was brought to the local black market to be sold. The money bought food that he took back home to his family. I believed the obviously poor lad, and took out a pack I had hidden in my sock and gave it to him. It made me feel good, and a carton of cigarettes only cost a dollar and ten cents at sea.

I met an American Coast Guardsman in civilian clothes assigned to a nearby station. He brought me to the military base club, where we spoke of home and the latest news. The mixed drinks were only twenty five cents for eight ounces of liquor, and free mixes of soda or juice. We left and had a great time talking, as he showed me the town's few highlights. We went to a local restaurant built on top of tall cement columns out over the ocean. The view of the horizon was breathtaking as the sun set right in front of us.

In the half glow of the sunset appeared a long line of rowing wooden boats. Each had a lit gas lantern on a tall pole hanging off the front bow. On either side of the pole were elevated huge round nets. As they came into focus, I saw each had a single man rowing out to sea. Every boat was tied to the next in a line as far as I could see, all rigged exactly alike. It looked like a string of weaving Chinese lanterns, that were slowly being rowed out of the harbor. The Coast Guardsman explained that each sunset they rowed out to catch flying fish that jumped up at the lights, and landed in their nets. The fish are flat and silvery, eight to ten inches long with pectoral fins a third the length of their bodies. They swim very fast, and to escape from being eaten, lock their fins and lift up out of the sea, gliding quite a distance using their tail as a rudder.

The next night, I had guard duty on deck and constantly had to kick flapping flying fish off our deck. They were attracted by our five hundred foot long strand of med lights.

Forty eight hours on this Italian island enjoying seven course meals, and old world charm was a wonderful two-day vacation. I consumed as many drinks as I could hold, and only spent five dollars on meals and drinks.

Our sub drove away from this paradise, leaving me with many great memories.

CHAPTER 25

Shark

Liberty on the Riviera was great, but that's not what we came here to do. In the early morning our sub left port and submerged, setting course to our new secret mission. We traveled very deep in ultra quiet mode, "we were a ghost in the ocean."

The captain passed the word "no unnecessary movement," so all that was allowed was performing our job or eating. Twenty-one steps from my bed to where I worked, or seven steps to eat. No showers were allowed in the 125-degree heat. It was 140 degrees at my work station, the power cubicle. I had to use rags to move the chrome power levers to prevent burning my hands. The large running main electric motors underneath my feet heated my room, till it was hard to breathe. I only stood a watch for a half hour with a safety rope tied around my waist; it got so hot I couldn't sweat. The rope would be used to pull me out if I passed out.

No labeled garbage could be shot out from our pointed down mini torpedo tube. This prevented depth charges from raining down on us, because of a piece of floating debris. Any labeled cigarette butts like Pall Mall, Camel, or stamped lids from cans and their wrappers would have shown an American presence.

The mess cook had to scrub off the *Sunkist* writing on the orange peels for later disposal. All non-labeled trash was brought amid ships to a small torpedo tube. Here weighted webbed trash bags were loaded, and when it was safe fired down into the ocean bottom. We stored the other garbage in webbed bags throughout our submarine even where we slept.

The heat became unbearable; it hurt to breathe through my nose, and I could only breathe through my mouth. We lay on our racks in just our underwear, bare-chested with legs spread apart, trying to cool down. We couldn't use our air conditioners, because they were noisy and used too much power. After two weeks on patrol, our main electric propulsion motors started to overheat. The eighty-five-degree sea water at two hundred feet wasn't cooling them down enough. One electrician constantly turned the dial, reading the motor temperatures. The safety circuits would shut them off at 180 degrees, and they were currently reading 179 degrees. We would quickly be a "sitting duck," if the motors tripped off and we floated to the surface. These electric motors are wound around the propeller shafts, and get power for propulsion from batteries when submerged or the sixteen cylinder main engine generators on the surface.

We were "never-there" was imperative.

In the Second World War, many submarines on both sides were detected by floating garbage picked up by local fishermen. The Germans or the U.S. tracked back along the currents, and sunk those submarines.

On some missions, we take pictures through the periscope camera of missile sites, installations, or vessels, and leave undetected. The executive officer develops the film behind a blanket in the ward room galley. I had no idea where we were or what was the mission. In the conning tower I heard things, but if I told you, they would eliminate us. We completed our task and left the area.

Finally away from the area, we surfaced. I felt the cool fresh air flow through the compartments. The smell of three weeks of fermenting garbage, in one hundred degree heat, slowly cleared. Now, it was my turn to freshen up with the long-awaited swim call.

Captain McFarland ordered "all stop," but kept the engines running. We were still at battle stations, and if detected, they would dive and leave us. He let half of the crew go swimming. I was lucky enough to be in the first group.

Swim Call Before Shark Attack

I took out my knife, shortened the legs of my jeans and dove in. Splash after splash sounded as each man took the plunge into the warm ocean, and rinsed off. It felt so good to get rid of the oily film from all over my body. Two men were posted as shark watches with M-1 rifles. All of our splashing can attract unwanted company. Someone threw a basketball out to us, and we played keep away with the officers. There were fifty enlisted men against five officers. We laughed and pushed the officers underwater any time they were near the ball. We were just one big family playing together as equals.

After splashing around for about a half hour, I heard someone scream "shark!" We all gathered together in a tight group floating with no movement. We were just less than two football-field-lengths away from the submarine. Any detected movement would be a lunch bell for sharks. We scanned around us looking for the normal small six-inch black shark fins. Instead, I saw a gigantic black fin well over a foot high followed by a saber-shaped fin far behind it. The look on everyone's face showed, *"we were in big trouble."* Our group was trapped in the open ocean by a huge great white shark. If the monster heard or felt any motion, he would zero in on us. Our previous splashing around, plus the engine exhaust was spraying out fishy smelling water from our bilge; this led him to the boat.

Our submarine looked and smelled like a huge black round whale, with wide black diving fins in the front and back.

The huge shark swam up against the sub's right side trying to bite off a piece of his new found whale. He circled counter clockwise raising and lowering his head time after time looking for a soft spot. We stared at him hoping he would realize the boat was not food. Time went by, one hour, then two, three and it got to be over six hours. The hungry shark still wouldn't leave, but kept circling trying to bite off something.

We were trapped just looking at this monster. if anyone panicked and took off, there would be a rolling blood bath for all. This is why the sub testing is so intense, keeping a cool head can save or kill lives all around you!

The captain yelled out to us, "it is going to be dark soon come in, or I will have to leave you here." The captain paused and said "he *can't eat you all*."

We now had no choice, but to swim in to the waiting shark. Huddled together, we waited till he swam around to the opposite side, then everyone quietly paddled toward our sub. After the shark swam around to the opposite side again, everyone swam toward the boat. When he came around the stern, the guys on deck yelled to us and we quickly formed back into a pod. The shark just kept swimming alongside the sub biting a higher or low spot, and would not leave.

Seeing the huge black fin go by in front of me, slowly turning his head from side-to-side, made me hold my breath. I wanted to run across the top of the water and get away. Every nerve in my body was on high alert. What to do against a school-bus-long animal thicker than the height of an off-road truck.

Finally, we were only a hundred feet away, and swam as fast as we could to the submarine. There was a major problem. There were fifty people in the water, and only one set of foot holes up the side onto the deck. The men rushed and grabbed through the eight-inch hand holes, pulling themselves up the side and throwing their bodies onto the deck.

A voice called out, "Here he comes." I was *one of twelve men* still waiting in the water. If I stayed I'd be lunch. I would also be detected if I swam out, and I'd be attacked. What to do? The Volkswagen-size head was coming right up the side at us.

The captain yelled down to us, "swim forward and stand on the diving planes." We swam and stood on the table-top size plane area, knee deep underwater. All twelve of us squeezed together, any detected movement by one, and all would suffer their fate.

The Great White swam toward us, and his cold black eyes stared right through me. His mouth opened wide showing his rows of teeth, and he swam just under my bare feet. When he cleared the diving planes, he quickly spun around lifting his head out of the water, just eight feet in front of me.

I wondered what he was thinking. Shall I have Polish, Italian, or French for lunch today? After a time, his head sunk below the surface in a swirl, and he swam back right under my feet. When he rounded the boat's stern, we nervously looked around and jumped back into the ocean. I swam as fast as I could to the foot holds, and climbed up onto the deck. Our shipmates laughed, and slapped our backs. They watched the entire event, but were helpless to do anything. Shooting would not kill the multi-ton shark, and his blood would bring other sharks.

In the past, we had caught sixteen-foot sharks on hooks using our mooring lines, and shot them with forty-five caliber pistols and Thompson sub-machine guns. It only made black marks on their skin," like putting out a cigarette." It couldn't penetrate. Only the armor piercing shells from the M1 rifle did the job. Shooting a shark the size of a kayak is one thing, but shooting a great white shark five feet shorter than a tour bus, with a bullet the size of a cigarette butt is quite another task.

God was with us that day.

I made a mistake by going to see the movie JAWS. It was no longer, a you missed me joke. JAWS made me relive the event over and over again. Now, I look all around for a while before going into the ocean, and swim away from him in my dreams, over and over each night!

Bow Planes

CHAPTER 26

Greece, Land of History

Our sub pulled into the fishing village port of Piraeus in southwestern Greece. It was a friendly town with smiling faces and a clear deepwater port. We could see many fish swimming below us, while backing up to the pier. Greece is a country full of history and artifacts, a dream come true for me from my high school days. The pictures on my foreign language books made me dream of faraway places.

I went to the town square in the hundred degree heat, and stood next to a dry fountain in the middle. All the roads were clean and in great shape, not like the previous countries that I visited. Everywhere about me was like a post card. Quaint stone buildings were on the shore, and in front of them were nets drying on poles next to multi-colored wooden boats. Each shop had a brightly colored sign hanging off the front in Greek, which I couldn't read. On the signs were pictures, "the universal language," and showed what each sold.

There was a bus stop sign showing Athens with an arrow. Soon, a bus pulled up and the driver opened a door for me. I said "Athens," and he motioned for me to come onboard. Holding out my hand full of Greek coins, the driver picked out two and put them in the meter. I was just riding along looking out the window at all types of artifacts, that were lying around on the hillsides unprotected. The bus stopped next to a subway station, and the sign read Athens with an arrow. Following the crowd down into the cool subway station, we boarded the modern subway and sped off. In no time, we arrived in Athens, and I followed the crowd up to the street.

Athens was an ultra-modern city rivaling New York City, but without sky scrapers. All streets were very wide and clear with curb stones and little newsstands on each street corner. The newsstands were filled with books, papers and snacks. Nearby was a museum with an intricately-carved, white marble entrance. Across the entire top of the entryway were scenes of men and horses engaged in battle. Inside, spread out before me was a vast hall filled with glass cases and doorways to multiple rooms. Looking into the glass cases were ancient helmets, shields, and swords, as their handles were long deteriorated by time. In another case were mummies of ancient Greeks encased in egg shaped pods. Their hands were tied in front of their knees in the fetal position. Everywhere stood statues and carvings from their great golden age. I was thrilled to see history come alive, just like the pictures in my high school history books.

Outside the museum, high up on a hill stood the Acropolis ruins. The Acropolis ruins were exactly like the cover of my Latin book. A spiral dirt road was the only access up to its entrance of the Temple Maiden Pillars. These 2500-year-old Virgins guarded the opening into the ruins courtyard. Passing through the arch into the courtyard, I looked through the ancient pillars at the city of Athens below. How many Greek soldiers had seen the same view thousands of years before me? I walked right on the ancient stones, worn smooth by leather sandals—here democracy started. The knowledge of the known world were written on scrolls by great scholars, and stored in a library nearby. Tales such as the voyage of the Iliad; there was so much history completely surrounding me. Reluctantly, I realized it was time to return down the hill path, passing by the closed iron gates of current expeditions digging under the pillars.

At the main square, I went up to shop owners for directions showing my small pad of paper with drawn ships and the ocean. No one understood the picture and this left me trapped in Athens, "everyone only speaks Greek!"

A bus pulled up across the street, and a shop owner pointed to him for directions. Waving at the bus he stopped, and opened the door for me. Relieved, I climbed up into the bus and said, "Piraeus." He responded, "Hello." Showing him the paper with boats and ocean on it, I asked was this the right bus to get there? He said, "Hello," again. I asked another question, still hello—the only English he knew. Motioning with my hands a wave action and pointing forward, the driver nodded. Going in one direction all the signs read Athens, which was the same spelling in both languages. I never thought of writing down the names of the towns we passed through. The bus headed for the setting sun, which eventually would get me to the ocean. Many bus stops later, we arrived in Piraeus. I was a very tired sailor, and wandered back to my boat. It was a matter of national pride to speak only the Greek language, a lesson I learned the hard way. Now, I knew what "an immigrant must feel like in AMERICA."

The next day was a working one. I solved electrical problems, and after supper started a battery charge. It took twelve hours to recharge the 252 main batteries, and the ship must be at full power. After working twenty-two straight hours in the heat, I collapsed onto my bed.

The next afternoon I went to the town square, and found a guide that spoke English. We made an agreement that I would buy him lunch, and pay five dollars for the day. We agreed to travel the least expensive way, and after my last experience I needed him. Men in this village commonly wait for work at the center of town for whatever work they can find. Working with the fishermen, handyman jobs, or farming was normal for him. We traveled by bus, subway or taxi to arrive at the Temple of Zeus, a must see for me. We walked right up and touched these ancient carved pillars. Reclining on one of the many broken down pillars, I discovered their secret. They were made up of a series of carved-circular wheels with a hole through the middle. The wheels were stacked high into columns with lead poured down through the center holes, forming a metal non rusting pole that held them up through the centuries.

My guide brought me to another ancient site where archaeologists were excavating. I could see statues and pots being stored behind a locked iron gate. The guide narrated about his culture and history with a broad smile, hand gestures and a twinkle in his eyes.

We walked down into town over an ancient dusty path for an authentic local meal. First, he went into the tiny restaurant and worked a deal with the owner. We had several great tasting local specials from soup to skewered meat. The meals were prepared and covered in special herbs cooked right in front of us on an open fire. The guide was pleased with my interest in his country's history, and willingness to try Greece's unique food. He brought me back to the fountain in Piraeus, and I gave him the five dollars and a little extra.

The next day our sub headed out for another secret mission, "I'd tell you where, but then I'd have to kill you." Just kidding, maybe!

Clearing the harbor, our submarine submerged down to one hundred feet and went to ultra-quiet. After cruising for many hours, we rose up to periscope depth, sixty-five feet and took pictures through the number one periscope. The camera was built right into the scope like the navigational tools. The executive officer developed these pictures in the ward room galley behind a blanket. The number two scope is two feet higher than number one, and has battle lines right on the lenses to judge height and distance to a target. The pictures developed ok, and we moved on to our next task. Finally, the mission was completed, and we headed out to open water and surfaced. The gentle roll of the Mediterranean Sea welcomed us back as the air rushed through the boat. Soon all the hardships of the mission were forgotten, and we looked forward to our time off. Just another mission three thousand miles from home, cruising through the waves with flying fish jumping around the bow.

CHAPTER **27**

Cuban Missile Crisis

We finished our mission in the Mediterranean Ocean, and headed out into the stormy North Atlantic, right into the teeth of hurricane ELLA. Our boat's round bottom made us roll radically from side to side in the storm's force. The violence of the wind and waves made me feel insignificant in the vastness of our swirling water-filled world. We left the hundred degree heat of the Mediterranean, and tried to adjust to the fifty degree waters of the North Atlantic. The USS Entemedor was a steel tube only twenty-seven feet wide. The hurricane flipped us about like a toy boat in the gale force waves. We were tossed high by the shrieking wind. We couldn't submerge, because we had less than a day's worth of air supply in our tiny tube with 125 men inside. This violent storm took three days for us to smash and crash through. In other hurricanes, I felt the waves forces three hundred feet down, as we slowly rocked back and forth with the hull making moaning sounds like a three-masted wooden ship.

Reality quickly set in when the waves raised the 2400-ton boat up, and smashed us down hard. I felt the boat shudder as she burst up and through a wave, twisting at once in many different directions. The crew shortened their bunk chains to create a forty-five degree angle, and placed their pillow against the outside hull. Being wedged in our bunks stopped us from beating our heads against the hull. Just walking in sync with the storm's motion became a full time job. I couldn't even open a hatch when the boat was rising, because its weight would knock me backwards to the deck. We all had black and blue marks on our arms and shins from hatch mishaps. Our leather shoes walking atop oil-soaked tile decks were the culprits, making us do a little dance when the boat slammed to one side unexpectedly.

We tied pencils on strings and hung them touching paper in three sections of the boat, which indicated the boat's reaction in the storm. The one in the forward torpedo room traced a long oval from front to back. The pencil amid ship traced a crazy eight pattern from side-to-side, and in the after torpedo room the pencil made an oval from side-to-side. These three different directions showed the force of the ocean against our tiny craft. Our hull was three quarters of an inch thick of high carbon steel—the width of your thumb, and the storm twisted our hull like soft taffy.

DAY ONE—The hurricane intensified until the white caps of the waves were blowing off the wave tops sideways. They looked like long white strands of straw. The mass volume of the waves became higher until they were almost one hundred feet tall. The roaring sounds made it imposable for the deck officer to communicate with the lookouts. Both lookouts were chained into their position by a six-inch-wide canvas belt with a four-inch-wide leather belt on top. The leather belt had three chains connected to the submarine, two forward and one aft. We were now far away from any land to block the wind and wave action.

DAY TWO—The waves grew till they were almost as high as the

width of a football field. Inside, everyone was tossed about without mercy. The three thousand pound propellers were breaking out of the waves, spinning wildly in the air. At the power cubicle, the two controller men had to constantly decrease and increase power to prevent the engines from over speeding and shutting down. When the propellers broke free, they vibrated the whole boat like putting your car in neutral at sixty mph.

I was one of those controller electricians standing with my legs wedged against the power cubicle. Both hands had to constantly turn the power wheels to control the generators and engine speed. My nerve endings got so tight, they played like a violin. Four hours of watching forty four gauges, and turning wheels every three to four minutes was exhausting. One mis-timed movement could shut down the engines, and the next wave could flip us over.

DAY THREE—The lookouts still rotated below every hour with their two counterparts. One lookout in the conning tower constantly turned the rudder trying to stay on course. The other hung on to the periscope looking for any targets through the high waves. The radar was useless from being buried underwater most of the time. Walking about was like walking across a trampoline, never knowing where the deck would be. The cook couldn't prepare meals, and brought buckets of sandwiches around to ease the hunger pangs.

DAY FOUR—I had the forward electrical watch in the middle of the submarine. I sat on a large heavy steel box tied down with rope. Over the speaker, I heard "Prepare for heavy waves." The words no sooner came out of his mouth as a rogue wave hit us broad side. We rolled radically to the right and kept going. Finally, we stopped at a fifty-seven degree angle and hung there. Fifty-four degrees was the "point of no return" for a submarine. We were supposed to keep turning till upside down. This would empty out all 9,072 gallons of acid from the batteries. If mixed with salt water, it formed chlorine gas. One whiff and you're dead.

The metal chest I sat on broke free, and started sliding across the deck with me in the air inches above it. My legs and arms were straight out, as I hit the opposite side and got tangled in a bunch of valve stems. Fortunately the chest hit just under me, before I fell down on top of it. The radical angle caused the oil in the running engines to drain out. The safety circuit shut the engines down, leaving us in total darkness. Hydraulic oil flowed all over the tiled deck, and my leather shoes slid beneath me. I felt my way along, crawling in the dark over pipes and cables. I found and turned on the power, letting the power cubicle switch to battery power. It immediately sent battery power to the main power cubicle, and the lights came on. They switched the main propulsion to battery power, and the propellers started to turn. We now had power to the rudder, and the sub slowly rose towards vertical. Extra weight had shifted to one side making it difficult to steer. It took a lot more power on one propeller, and full rudder to bring the submarine upright. Back in the berthing area all thirty-six bunks had broken off their supports, and dropped into a pile with the deck heaters. This created a hot thirty-six man sandwich twisted together with broken chains and blankets.

The auxiliary man looked at me and started to laugh. The side of my face and arms were covered with black and blue half inch circles all down one side of my body. It happened when I was flying across the deck into the valve stems. We had a nervous laugh together before returning to repair the storm damage. Moving about was like a hockey game, sliding on oil soaked decks in heavy seas.

Our sister submarine had traveled across with us, but was not as lucky as we were. When they went up to relieve the topside watches, the officer was hanging onto the binocular stand, and one lookout was hanging by his chains over the side. The lookout on the other side was missing, only broken chains hung where he was.

The submarine was tossed and spun around for two more days, till I no longer could identify up from down. I was feeling seasick. Still very hungry after days without food, I made a big mistake. I made a rib sticking peanut butter sandwich; hunger overcame my common sense. The Velcro-like sandwich slowly moved up my throat and erupted. I felt like I was going to turn inside out, and deeply regretted my choice. Only one chief engine man didn't get sick out of the 125 member crew. Everyone had a container nearby for our many volcanic eruptions. The storm numbed our internal balance, and if asked to point left or right, up or down—I had to stop and figure it out.

DAY FIVE—The submarine finally broke out of the main hurricane, and we slowed down to repair damage. We crawled along the whole day, which seemed strange because we were all anxious to return home.

DAY SIX TO EIGHT—We continued to rock and roll in the open Atlantic. On day eight, the crew asked to connect the radio to an antenna but we were refused. The radio was normally tuned to AM Channel 1010 Winds, New York the strongest am signal. When we are about 350 miles from land we hear the chimes, 1010 Winds, New York. The whole crew would cheer loudly, knowing we were close to home.

DAY NINE—Chief Charwinski was the head of all the electricians and my boss. I was sleeping when the Chief came to me and said, "Order spare parts for everything electrical on board."

I said laughingly, "ha ha, nice joke." He said, "I'm not fooling."

Ordering spare parts was just one of my many electrical duties. Thinking of the hundreds of parts needed, I dreaded the task. I went to the mess hall with stacks of seven-layer order forms. I started printing from the multiple spare part lists. I pressed down, writing on all of the carbon layers till I couldn't feel my hands. I wrote non-stop for hours, then took a short break and continued. After thirty-six hours of no sleep, I ended with two stacks of order forms each about two feet high. I jumped into my bunk and passed out for a few hours. I awoke by the sound of the battle alarm bonging over and over. Everyone ran to their battle station and stood by. We waited for the drill to be over, but this was not a drill.

I saw two sailors walk through the boat armed—one with a machine gun, and the other with a forty-five pistol. We joked, "How could anyone shoot a machine gun surrounded by high pressure lines, electronic gear, and electrical cables?"

We headed up the Thames River Channel with armed men topside and below decks at battle stations. I was ordered to get my forms ready and soon the sub backed up, facing out to sea next to the Submarine Tender USS Fulton AS11. I went to a waiting jeep with an armed driver, and drove off through the main gate guarded by Marines with machine guns. The Marines returned shoulder-to-shoulder, as we headed towards the main submarine base. There, our jeep was escorted to the main supply building, where I dropped off the order forms. By the time I returned to the Fulton, there were two lines of sailors loading food down our hatches. Live torpedoes were lowered down through the small middle center hatches. I still didn't know what was going on, but I thought we were at war. Everywhere I looked, I saw armed marines and sailors prepared for action at a moment's notice.

The end of the day arrived and all the other submarines still had their engines running at battle stations. Only two lines tied each of the submarines together, instead of the normal four. We were not allowed to hear the radio or have any outside contact. The Cold War Era atmosphere left us waiting to hear if we were at war. The engines rumbled all through the night till morning. We secured from battle stations and the married men were allowed to leave the submarine for four hours. They had to keep in contact with the boat, but the rest of us were not allowed to leave. We had no radio to find out what was going on. When the married men returned, we found out about the Cuban Missile Crisis. We sat on top of the extra food stored everywhere. At the end of the next day, the rest of us were allowed to go into town for a few hours. I had to keep in contact with the submarine, and stay in the nearby town. The following day all seemed to quiet down, and we were allowed to leave overnight. We had to stay within a one-hour return drive.

Normally, we are not supposed to drive for twenty-four hours after a long trip. We lose our depth perception from never being more than twenty-five feet from a wall. When driving a car, you turn too soon and havoc ensues. We had one married sailor who totaled his car trying to drive home after a long trip. He borrowed his wife's car to get back, and totaled that one too.

I think back to the day and a half, that we slowly traveled in the Atlantic. This was the time period, which top brass probably was deciding what direction to send us. New London, Connecticut is the northernmost submarine base, and the first line of defense. Russian ships had to get through a narrowing to get out into the Atlantic. We were already close to that spot, and would have to stop them from coming through. We had a few live torpedoes and some food left, it would have been difficult to go into battle with so little.

During the early sixties, we were told Russia had 550 submarines on the East Coast, and we only had sixty-five. The U.S. gave WW II diesel submarines to the Russians after the Second World War, and this made me nervous. They looked interchangeable with ours at sea, and have the same underwater sound signature and capabilities. Some Russian submarines had their forward deck cut off, and mounted two missiles. All they had to do was surface high enough to fire the missiles under the radar lower limit.

All of the rest of the world is still building diesel submarines except the UNITED STATES, and they are much cheaper than nuclear submarines. With other old-time submariners, I had a private tour of the newest nuclear submarine—the USS New Hampshire. We were told it was still very hard to find a diesel submarine.

In 2009, a Scottish diesel submarine operated with the Pacific Fleet for a year, and was never found during the many war games. The Scottish diesel submarine had power cells instead of batteries, and stayed submerged for many weeks without recharging. The recharging on the surface accounted for most submarines being sunk in World War II.

The Cold War was a scary time for all. If the action on either side was misunderstood, all life as we know it would have changed forever!

CPSIA information can be obtained at www.ICGtesting.com
Printed in the USA
BVOW02s0106140115

383186BV00009B/134/P